Ann Marie Woodall

secrets of
a high-heeled
healer

How to Find Purpose,
Passion and Adventure

Element
An Imprint of HarperCollins*Publishers*
77-85 Fulham Palace Road,
Hammersmith, London W6 8JB

The website address is: www.thorsonselement.com

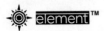

and *Element* are trademarks of
HarperCollins*Publishers* Ltd

First published by Element 2003

10 9 8 7 6 5 4 3 2 1

A catalogue record of this book is
available from the British Library

ISBN 0 00 714925 5

Printed and bound in Great Britain by
Martins The Printers Ltd, Berwick upon Tweed

contents

dedication

I dedicate this book to my children Maxyne C. Ryan
and Roger Woodall Jnr

acknowledgements

In the production of this book, I am indebted to numerous people, far too many to mention by name, and I truly thank you *all*. I would like to thank in particular 'Woody', my partner, for all the endless cups of tea, day and night; George and Marie Hyland, my mum and dad; Julie, Gina, Kevin, Eddie and Veronica, my brothers and sisters; Dr David Prendergast, my nephew; Nick Williams, a good friend; Chuck and Lensy Spezzano, for showing me another way; Jackee Holder, for her energy; Jenny Ridley, Linda Nichols, Suzanne Sullivan, Tania Woodward and Jonathan Boxer, the 'Travelling Healerettes'; Julia McCutchen, who brought every fibre of this book together; Rose Desmier and Sally Goodwin, who made sense out of the chapters; Paul and Isobel Manweiler, for believing in me; and Veronica Hyland, my sister through time, for all the hours of love, support and impeccable insight. You are definitely the wind beneath my wings.

secrets of finding purpose, passion and adventure

Never regret. If it's good, it's wonderful. If it's bad, it's experience.
VICTORIA HOLT

I am asked regularly how I got a name like 'the High-Heeled Healer'. Well, here's the story. Brita Dhalberg, a powerful businesswoman based in Germany, invited me to facilitate a workshop at the Frankfurter Ring, a company that had been in business for over 30 years promoting speakers and teachers from around the world. For that particular weekend I had bought myself a beautiful azure blue silk suit with a great pair of matching shoes.

After I'd been speaking to the group for about an hour, it was time for a break. A few of the participants came up to me to ask questions. Among them was a large well-dressed Fräulein with a quizzical look on her soft, rounded face. 'May I speak to you?' she said, 'I have attended many lectures over *ze* past 15 years and met many speakers from all over *ze* world. I would like you to know you really inspired me *zis* evening, but I have to tell you something – in all those years I have never seen *ze* healer in high heels!'

I laughed nervously and wondered whether this was a compliment or an expression of real concern. Then it dawned on me that it was a heaven-sent gift. Everyone we encounter has a role to play in our lives and a message that would help us on our way if we but had the ears to hear it. This was one of those messages. From that day on I became known as 'the High-Heeled Healer'.

In fact the shoes became the symbol of a whole new style of healing. High-heeled healers play, laugh, flirt and enjoy a good glass of wine. They love what they do and they share their knowledge of love, life and healing with a high level of enthusiasm and a potent draught of passion. They see the sacred in the small and the silly things as well as the sad. They rebel against heartache, fear and self-attack. *You can't play small when you're wearing four-inch heels!*

Anyone can learn high-heeled healing – and discover the secrets of purpose, passion and adventure along the way. I wrote this book to show you how. You don't need years of chanting on a mountain top, a large Swiss bank account or a month's supply of shrink-wrapped Valium sandwiches. All you need is a willingness to take one small (high-heeled) step at a time on an adventurous journey within.

It's a fascinating, scary and hilarious journey. Like most people, it's a journey that I managed to avoid for years while I was busy looking for fulfilment in all the wrong places. But after 38 years, two children, two husbands, five careers, eight homes, ten cars, 752 bottles of champagne, 4,352 Hail Marys and one mad Shirley Valentine moment, I still wasn't happy.

☆ the *S*hirley Valentine experience

Sometimes I think, 'Did that really happen in my life or was it just a dream?' Eager for fun and adventure, at 20 years old I left Manchester for the bright lights of London. I found exactly what I was looking for at the famous Playboy Club where I trained as a croupier bunny. Dealing Black Jack, roulette and Punto Banco to some of the world's richest, most glamorous and most influential high-rollers, I played and partied the night away at the most exclusive night-clubs, bars and restaurants with rock stars and millionaires. Life was fast, exciting and very colourful.

Then one fine day I hung up my pristine velvet bunny ears, soft white powder-puff tail and kicked off my shiny red four-inch heels for the last time. Yes, I was in love and I was off to marry my dream guy. Not a high-roller or a millionaire, but a kind, honest, good man. We worked hard for years running a successful business together and had two beautiful children. And all along we tried our best to maintain the romance of that first kiss. And then ...

What happened to Shirley Valentine? She got married to a boy called Joe. And somewhere along the way Joe turned into him and she turned into this. And what I can't remember is the day, the week, or the month when it happened, when it stopped being so good. Shirley Valentine disappeared and became just another name on the missing person list.
WILLY RUSSELL

Watching Willy Russell's West End play *Shirley Valentine* some years ago it really hit home to me how many of Shirley's struggles had been mine. Shirley had spent the last few years talking to the kitchen wall. She was good at dealing with things that showed no sign of life – like her husband and her marriage. After 14 years, my marriage was in a similar state, though I tried all kinds of things to revive it. I manipulated, I cried, I feigned illness. I worked hard alongside my husband in our business. I tried being 'super-housewife'. I lost lots of weight and worked out. I even had an affair, just to make him jealous. Nothing worked.

Finally I decided to 'do a Shirley': I booked a place on a Caribbean cruise and ended up in Brazil. Sitting on a fluffy cerise towel on one of the most exotic beaches in the world with a glass of wine in my hand and my credit cards smouldering through excessive use, I thought, 'This is *bound* to get his attention.' Unfortunately, I was not alone on the towel. My husband, my kids, my mum and dad, my sisters and brothers, my memories, dreams, hurt, sadness and disappointment were all there with me. The scenery on the outside may have changed but the world inside me hadn't. I began to realize that no matter where I ran, I would take my life with me.

At least I did succeed in getting my husband's attention – but not in the way I'd expected. Within a week of my return to England he called me to say that he'd met a blonde, 15 years his junior and now pregnant! As I put down the phone I fell to my knees and howled. I was fearful, guilty, lonely and afraid of the future. My old life had disappeared in one short phone call and what was ahead of me now? I didn't even really know who I was any more. Like so many women, I'd played many roles – mother, wife, business partner – and lost myself along the way.

looking for answers in all the wrong places

As the months went by, I started searching for answers – any answers. I visited tarot readers of dubious intent, psychics who used whistles, bells and chanting to invoke a spirit or two, big buxom ladies in purple cheesecloth reading crystal balls, tea leaves and palms. I attended séances, but the dead didn't seem to have the answers either. How about astrology? Should I look for a Leo or a Virgo? Was it just all a 'no-go'?

I didn't get many answers from my motley band of mystics and I didn't get many from my friends either, though we had few 'post-traumatic pity parties' where we all had a good old-fashioned moan. But eventually the pity got really boring, even to me. What was I going to do? I wanted to run away again, but I was still paying off the credit cards from last time.

At this, my lowest ebb, I prayed. I prayed to heaven for guidance. I needed help. For the first time, I was truly praying from the heart. I prayed for a teacher, a friend who would be able to guide, motivate and inspire me. I wanted to understand my emotions, my behaviour, to understand what made me tick. I wanted to find out who I was – to be real, to be authentic.

the high-heeled healer's dream

Answers come in many forms when you are on a healing path. Mine came as a most unusual dream ...

In my dream, a group of angels in heaven were snuggled into large, soft, light blue, gold and pink marshmallow clouds, all dreaming of going back to earth, and I was one of them. From below, we heard a cry for help: *'There's got to be more to life than this.'* This cry was our alarm call.

A delicately glowing lilac light gently approached our heavenly sanctuary and told us: 'When you go back to earth, remember:

* remember to enjoy yourselves
* remember you will always have a connection to heaven
* remember you volunteered to help.'

We all smiled at each other. *'As if we could forget!'*

Lined up preparing to leave, we were told that we would need protection on earth, so before handing in our wings we put on some SPF – soul protection factor – made up of accountability and choice.

Accountability is actually a key part of high-heeled healing. It means looking at life from a higher perspective, taking complete responsibility for all our thoughts and deeds in every area of our lives. This may sound like a heavy deal, but in fact accountability is freeing. It allows you to look for the lessons in life's dramas. As for choice, you can use choice to move through any sticky situation. Whatever you do and wherever you go, there is always choice.

Back in the dream all the volunteers for 'Assignment Earth' lined up and off we went to the Great Akashic Palace. Inside there were two very large ornate books made from the finest rainbow silk and fairies' sparkle. From the pages of the bigger book we each picked our mother and father for the coming lifetime. From the second book, we could choose some brothers and sisters too.

Then on we went to the Gift Shop. This was a special shop. It was huge.
As we went in, we were issued with Spiritual Backpacks. These could hold
as many gifts as we wanted to carry on this trip. We were told that the
gifts were heaven's tools for transformation. Our purpose was to share
them with everyone we met on earth and to remember that our lives
were a spiritual journey towards the realization that we are *love*. We were
told that the world had fallen into a deep sleep, but that as soon as you
gave a heavenly gift to someone they would start to wake up and
remember. We could choose a special gift for each member of our new
earth family. And we could pack gifts to heal the planet itself. When on
earth, if at any time we needed more gifts, all we had to do was remember
our spiritual connection.

Smiling, we told each other that we would never, never forget our
connection and never ever, ever forget our purpose. Then we jumped ...
and landed on earth with one massive great big bang.
'Where the hell am I?'
'What am I doing here?'
Amnesia set in ...

This dream stayed with me for weeks and I kept mulling it over in my
mind. Could all these things somehow be true? Then, as I started looking
for a better way to live, I discovered that most of the principles put
forward by the major religions of the world, the great philosophers and
mystics are similar. They all speak about giftedness, choice and connecting
to heaven, exactly like my dream. Throughout our journey together in
these chapters, these ideas will be a recurring theme, a golden thread of
Truth. From this small thread we can pull our lives together again.

from mess to mystic

After this, I spent many years studying, researching and *living* the latest
ideas about success and personal fulfilment. My first port of call was a
Buddhist centre, where I learnt to chant. Then I undertook a number of

short courses in the psychology of transformation and enrolled on a five-year programme studying the 'Psychology of Vision', based on the teachings of *A Course in Miracles* and cutting-edge psychological research into relationships and spirituality. The course was fascinating and led me on to further research into NLP (neuro-linguistic programming), hypnotherapy and life coaching. From the deserts of New Mexico to the high mountains of Canada gifted shamans passed on their knowledge of energy healing and dream work, and experts in conflict resolution shared their skills. These were all very powerful models of transformation and I finally felt I was getting closer to the answers I'd been searching for. And in one of my most inspired moments, I decided to integrate all the teachings I'd absorbed into a method of personal transformation that was fun and could be easily understood by anyone.

I want to mention here that these principles are not my invention. They are not new, they are based on ancient teachings and universal laws. But most of all, they are fun! Some years ago, I discovered that barriers to change can best be broken down by humour and curiosity. The first workshops I ran required a sense of humour – as well as a sarong and a swimsuit! They were called 'the Shirley Valentine Experience' and were for anyone who had ever felt like running away. Throughout this book we will be looking at what we might want to run away from – and how instead we can set out on a journey to find the secrets of success.

☆ how to use this book

You already have all the guidance you could ever want inside you. This book will teach you how to connect to it through the most powerful part of your mind – what I term the 'Miracle Mind' (although you may prefer to think of it as trust or intuition or something similar). Through it, you can start to answer any question you have about your life and its purpose. Magic and miracles are not just the imaginings of a bygone age; they are real and available to us here and now. All you need do is be open to the power of grace, energy, creative force and soul-level power working on your behalf. It's the quickest way to find purpose, passion and adventure, and you know what, this magical force has the most incredible sense of humour! You'll start to discover this while you're working through this book.

There is a divinity that shapes our ends, rough-hew them how we will.
WILLIAM SHAKESPEARE

You may have already come across the term 'synchronicity', a concept developed by Jung which has become more popular recently with books such as James Redfield's *The Celestine Prophecy*. This is the theory that we are given signs by the universe all the time but often we are blind to them. We get so wrapped up in the past and what we *think* was true that we can't see the exciting future that's trying to unfold in front of us. Over the next seven chapters you will discover how to read those signs and shape that future. You will learn how to:

- ✶ reconnect and use the most powerful part of your mind
- ✶ discover your wonderful hidden gifts
- ✶ check out of Heartbreak Hotel
- ✶ recognize the traps, tricks and temptations that sabotage relationships
- ✶ understand more about the 'f' words – failure, fear and forgiveness
- ✶ loosen up, lighten up and laugh again
- ✶ realize that adventure and life purpose are one.

You'll find tools to help you fine-tune your approach to vitality, happiness, peace, love, relationships, success and creativity, including exercises, journal work and meditations as well as fun suggestions.

the 'For your Eyes Only' journal

The idea of journal work is not new but the benefits are truly tried and tested. Confidential journals have been written through the ages. Writing a journal is like speaking to a cherished friend who does not judge or try to fix you – a friend who helps you clarify your thoughts, who listens to your fears and doubts. It is an inventive way to clear issues from the past. Let your thoughts be liberated onto paper!

The first step is to buy yourself an A4 notebook; this is your 'For your Eyes Only Journal'. You could customize it – envelop it in rich velvet, swathe it in lace or wrap it in satin. You could cover it in a collage of your dreams or adventures – it's entirely up to you. I know when I customize my journals they each take on their own uniqueness; a new part of me has shown up.

Your journal is a place to draw, doodle and dream. At first you may find that you are still writing in it as though somebody else will read it. Don't. Write everything down in an uncensored way, no matter how strange or socially inappropriate. Remember it is your private journal. It's *'For your Eyes Only'*. Keep it in a safe place.

Use your journal at any time to write your wish lists, jot down your feelings, create collages, scribble or crayon. Invite your intuitive mind to come out and play. You'll soon start to surprise yourself. Write what is *really* in your heart. Be radically honest with yourself. You can't change if you keep fooling yourself.

Every morning, if possible, give yourself ten minutes to clear your mind of any thoughts hanging over from the previous day, worries about the coming day or details of your night-time dreams. Then write down a goal for the day on an index card or somewhere safe and keep it with you all day to remind yourself of it.

At the end of the day try to take just ten minutes to make a list in your journal of what was better or worse about that day and what worked for you. This gets your mind off your problems and on to a path of growth.

As you realize how much power you have to create your own life, you will start to make new choices in many areas. Writing them down starts the process of manifesting or attracting what you want in your life.

healerette's happy hours

At the end of each chapter there will also be tips and ideas of how to be spontaneous, playful and even silly. These suggestions are just as important as the more 'serious' ones that precede them. They will ask you to take an hour, perhaps three times a week, of private time to pamper yourself at little cost. Your homework is to lighten up, loosen up and laugh at yourself. I am giving you permission to be as spontaneous, selfish, sassy and abandoned as you want. This is sometimes the hardest part of the process because it requires making an effort just for yourself. But one of the High-Heeled Healer's favourite mantras is that life is meant to be fun!

So now let's get started. Open up to the magic of life – it worked for me and it works for everyone. New attitudes lead to new possibilities. There is no limit to your purpose, passion and adventure!

Chapter One

miracles

Creating a new theory is not like destroying an old barn and erecting a skyscraper in its place. It is rather like climbing a mountain, gaining new and wider views, discovering unexpected connections between our starting points and its rich environment. But the point from which we started out still exists and can be seen, although it appears smaller and forms a tiny part of our broad view gained by the mastery of the obstacles on our adventurous way up.
ALBERT EINSTEIN

What a wonderful vision of life Albert Einstein had. It fits in perfectly with the sentiments expressed in this book. After all, who would know more about how to find purpose, passion and adventure than one of the world's great geniuses? Legend has it that Albert first worked out the theory of relativity while he was sleeping. He dreamt that he was riding on a beam of light and suddenly the famous formula for his theory of relativity flashed into his mind: $e=mc^2$. Now that's what I call a miracle!

The secret of Albert's genius is that he was able to access an extraordinary part of the human mind. It's the part that simply receives. It doesn't struggle, plot or try to figure things out. It lets in dreams, intuitions and sudden inspirations. It guides our creativity and inspires our search for adventure. I call it the 'Miracle Mind'.

Your Miracle Mind contains a great big Spiritual Backpack full of high-level gifts that you can use to transform any situation and find any answers you need. In this chapter, we'll look at where the Miracle part of our Mind comes from and how to use it just like Einstein did. But first we need to get a handle on how the human mind generally works and why it sometimes feels as though it's better at getting us into trouble than getting us out of it.

☆ meet your split mind

Man versus Man.
Man versus Nature.
Man versus Himself.
ANON

Albert Einstein was inspired, playful and kind-hearted, and he wasn't afraid of his giftedness – all signs of a true Miracle Minder. Albert had a great sense of humour too. He knew that life was meant to be happy and that we weren't supposed to take things as seriously as we all do. We're not supposed to be stuck with our problems. Yet somehow we grow up to take everything *sooo* seriously because we think that's what adults are supposed to do. It's a belief that begins very early in life and it comes from what is known as 'the split mind'. Everybody has one.

It goes like this: on entry into this planet we are innocent, shiny, angelic little beings fresh from a fluffy cloud in heaven (or whatever spiritual equivalent you choose to believe in). Until now, all we have known is *love*. When we arrive on the planet we are full of love. There's nothing to worry about and nowhere to go. We just lie back and receive – just as Einstein did. It's miraculous! We are fed, watered and loved to the best of our parents' or carers' ability. All we have to do in return is smile and gurgle a few times. Then the harsh day comes when nobody comes running *immediately* in response to our every whim. The reason for it may be something so simple, so understandable that as adults we wouldn't think it mattered. Maybe someone's at the door or big brother is having a tantrum. However, as babies, the feeling of separation we have just encountered is dramatic and we start to think that we are on our own.

Gradually, we start to think that maybe being open, loving, innocent and as cute as can be isn't enough any more. Maybe life isn't so safe and easy after all. Maybe we're wrong about people loving us too? A little bit of doubt creeps into our minds and for the first time we feel a level of fear. Our mind has split. Half of it believes in love, but the other half now believes in fear. Thinkers, mystics and psychologists throughout the ages have coined many terms for this psychological crisis, but I call these parts of our mind the 'Miracle Mind' (love) and the 'Ego Dramatist' (fear).

The Miracle Mind is the true source of our power. It remembers we are gifted and have a connection to heaven. In fact, in partnership with our hearts, the Miracle Mind *is* our connection to heaven. The Miracle Mind comes from a place of bonding, luck, manifesting, trust and intuition. It comes from love. However, the Ego Dramatist is suffering from spiritual amnesia. It doubts we have any connection to heaven and thinks we are alone in this world. The Ego Dramatist comes from fear. It believes in lack – not enough money, not enough love, not enough support, not enough time. It's always looking and never seems to find.

So, from the earliest age, our minds are split. Some lucky people grow up surrounded by enough love and security to carry on believing in the Miracle Mind and trusting to that better side for most of their life. They are the ones you probably look at with envy and think, 'Why do they have such an easy life?' Unfortunately, most of us end up paying more attention to our Ego Dramatist.

☆ are you a miracle minder or an ego dramatist?

You'll know which part of your mind you've been using by how you are feeling. Your Miracle Mind will bring you health, wealth and all the things you desire in your wildest and most outrageous dreams. Your Ego Dramatist will bring you moans, groans and a large collection of final straws!

Miracle Minders feel loved, peaceful and connected to the people around them. Miracle Minders create the most amazing, marvellous, dynamic life, full of pleasant surprises. They make those around them feel happier. People want Miracle Minders to succeed and will give them help along their path of adventure. Days of Miracle Mindedness are full of harmony, inside and out. Miracle Minders are very good for our world. They instil a sense of possibility against all odds.

Ego Dramatists feel stressed and depressed, lost and alone. Their lives unfold like a soap opera with major sagas of tragedy, trauma and struggle. Their approach to others is often to reject, complain, criticize and control. If life were a game of snakes and ladders, they would always land on the snake. Sometimes they won't play at all. People let them down, plans go awry and change feels impossible. The Ego Dramatists' way of achieving anything is always the hard way: busy, busy, burnout. Ego Dramatists wake up and fall asleep with their fears.

In fact, most of us are constantly shifting from one part of our mind to the other. The secret is to start using and trusting your Miracle Mind more often on a regular basis, and then, with time, your whole attitude to life will start to change. Miracles will happen.

A miracle is a shift in perception. There is no order or size of difficulty.
A COURSE IN MIRACLES

☆ what's your racket?

So, do you want the good news or the bad news? OK, first the bad news. Let's get it over with. Once the mind splits it carries on splitting every time we come from the place of fear and separation (our Ego Dramatist). Our originally open and innocent mind ends up so full of fractures that it starts to look more like a tennis racket than a clear, open, loving and receiving space.

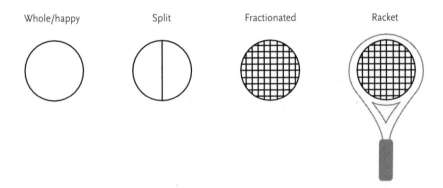

| Whole/happy | Split | Fractionated | Racket |

Each string on that mental memory racket represents a piece of our past, a feeling of loss, hurt, abandonment, rejection, heartbreak. There are all kinds of juicy grievances in there, the biggest one being that our mother/father/brothers/sisters/aunts/uncles/next-door neighbours/cats/dogs/favourite teachers didn't love us just exactly the way we wanted – they only loved us as well as they could.

Everybody in the world, from gangsters to gurus, has one of these rackets. When I first developed the idea it made me laugh to think that everyone we meet, rich or poor, old or young, man or woman, has a racket neatly hidden somewhere about their person. But the way we use our rackets isn't funny. Rather than just cut the strings and let the painful emotions go, we save them up and use them as ammunition to keep people at arm's length. Most of the time, we don't even know that we're doing it. But we do know that the once great adventure of life has become limited and boring. Does this ring any bells with you?

Audrey Hepburn: Are you making a pass at me?
Cary Grant: Well, I…
Audrey Hepburn: Because I already know far too many people and until somebody dies I couldn't possibly know any more.
FROM THE 1964 FILM *Charade*

Eventually we're holding on to so many mistakes, misunderstandings, hurts and grievances that we've no room for any more people or fresh adventures. We stop taking risks and we start to close down. Yes, we do have moments of inspiration, yet more often than not we don't make the move to change or transform ourselves because the Ego Dramatist has persuaded us that it's not going to work, so why bother? We stop living our lives and start trying to 'handle' them.

To protect ourselves from perceived hurts and hazards, when people start to get a little too close we pull out our rackets and whack them with the full force of all that buried childhood pain:

★ 'If I cheat on you before you cheat on me, it won't hurt when you abandon me like everyone else (so I think I'll sleep with your best friend).' Whack!
★ 'You sound exactly like my father (and you know how much he annoys me).' Wallop!
★ 'Eat! I've been up all night cooking for you. Eat! (I'll never forgive myself for the cold you caught when you were three – I'm a terrible mother.)' Thunk!

It doesn't take us long to become expert at using our rackets. We can whack people so quickly (and discreetly) that they don't know what's hit them. Then we sit on our hands, hum at the sky and make like a martyr or smile the most winning smile in our armoury. If all else fails, we pick a fight to make our 'opponent' feel guilty. Guilt will glue them to the floor – but we will be stuck in the impasse too.

exploring your racket

Rather than helping us, our rackets always end up pushing what we want away from us. We push people away, love away, success away and money away. Not good. Are you ready to clean up your racket?

In Switzerland I was working with a group of businessmen who were all very efficient workers and keen sportsmen. They were all from different backgrounds: some were rich and had attended exclusive seminars and others were working-class boys whose parents had worked extremely hard to get the best education for them.

On the second day we were discussing patterns and belief systems. I asked them what their parents' beliefs had been about money. To my surprise, the rich guys said that although their parents had had money there was always the underlying fear that they might lose it, so they had to be careful with it.

The guys from the poorer backgrounds said that their parents had had exactly the same fears about money, but this was because they had none and had to be extremely careful too.

The fear was exactly the same – whether you are rich or poor, you still have a racket.

Now it's time for the good news: rackets aren't the only thing we're hiding behind our backs. Remember the Spiritual Backpacks in my dream? In these we carry all the gifts we could possibly need to provide the antidote to every difficulty, crisis or dilemma we face. There are hundreds of gifts in there. They come straight from your Miracle Mind.

Your Miracle Mind's purpose is to help you clear your racket enough to *live the life you want* – to be free, to feel good, to be healthy, loving, successful and creative, to be inspired and, ultimately, to drop the racket altogether. Remember, you are *accountable* and you are in charge at all times. You can *choose* whether to heal a problem or remain in pain.

Your Miracle Mind is always available and very willing to heal these difficult areas, so with a little curiosity and a lot of love, let's find out what's in your racket.

Let's work with your journal for this first exercise. And remember, it's 'For your Eyes Only', so be as honest as you can bear. This is a particularly good exercise to do if you are feeling overwhelmed by demands or if your life seems stagnant and restricted.

- First, make a list of all the people you are having difficulties with at the moment. Go for the big ones. Write down their names.
- Add to the list anyone you're feeling hurt by, anyone you find yourself constantly criticizing, anyone you'd like to see a whole lot less of.
- Note down people you haven't forgiven, people who haven't forgiven you. You're aiming to make a complete list of all those relationships that 'could do better'.
- Now draw a big picture of a tennis racket, just like in the diagram. Add a string for every person on your list and write their name on it.
- Finished? What you've just drawn is a diagram of how much you are holding on to from the past.
- How are you doing? Are you totally clogged up or reasonably clear?
- Don't worry if your racket is looking very cluttered. It just means that you have plenty of potential locked away which, when unleashed, will increase your energy and open you up to receive some really good things in your life.

clearing your racket

Knowing is not enough; we must apply. Willing is not enough; we must do.
JOHANN WOLFGANG VON GOETHE

As Goethe says, knowing and willing are not enough. It's time to do it. Let's start clearing your racket.

First, we're going to work with the biggest name on your list — the one that is taking up most of your energy at the moment. What is the feeling that comes up when you think of this person? Hurt, anger, confusion, betrayal? Name it. We're going to do a simple question-and-answer exercise to help you start clearing it. Edna Brillon, a very good friend of mine, taught me this simple exercise during an Extraordinary Life Coaching seminar in Canada. It's called 'Could You, Would You, When?'

★ *Could you?* means you have probably done something similar before and you know are capable of doing it again.
★ *Would you?* means you are willing and able.
★ *When?* means 'In what time frame?'

Using these five words to clear your 'racket' is so simple yet effective.

The top name in Fiona's racket was her ex-boyfriend Michael. The feeling she associated with him was betrayal. I asked her to feel the emotion of the betrayal, which she did easily. I then asked:

★ '*Could you* let it go?' After some serious thought she admitted: 'Yes.'
★ '*Would you* let it go?' Again, 'Yes.'
★ '*When?*' 'In two weeks.'

As soon as she'd said this, Fiona was amazed she was choosing to hold on to that pain for two more weeks. We repeated the exercise four times, until she decided she would let the feeling go *right now*. As she left the office, she looked ten years younger. Two weeks later, she phoned to say that she had been teaching her friends how to do the exercise and she hadn't felt so vital and vibrant in years. It felt so good to let go. (And so much cheaper than Botox!)

Do this exercise when you have at least 20 minutes to spare:

- What feeling you do associate with the top name on your list?
- *Could you* let it go?
- *Would you* let it go?
- *When?*

Repeat this exercise four or more times until you feel at peace. You could ask a friend to help you. Have a happy healing session together. You don't have to explain any story or spend hours going through an event in your mind. Just feel the emotion, feel where it is held in the body, and then do the exercise.

choosing your gift

Remember in the High-Heeled Healer's dream the importance of protecting your soul through accountability and choice? Well, that last exercise was about accountability and this exercise is all about choice.

- What gift are you ready to receive in place of that old emotion? Fiona found a whole new level of vitality and understanding. Once she'd let go of her ex-boyfriend she felt ready to trust men again.
- Now remember in the dream when we chose our parents, our brothers and sisters, and filled our Spiritual Backpack full of gifts, talents and creativity? What were the gifts you brought to your family?
- What is the talent you have that you are not using?
- What project have you always wanted to do and have never started? *Now* is the time.

if it's good enough for Einstein ...

Remember the quote from Einstein at the start of the chapter? You too can gain 'new and wider views'. Take a view of life from a higher plane and rediscover yourself through a simple shift in perception. Choose to let go of the past and create a life of miracles.

☆ healerette's happy hour

Finally, it's time to pamper yourself. Remember, one of the High-Heeled Healer's key mantras is that life is meant to be fun!

cashmere blanket meditation

The following exercise will help you to connect to your Miracle Mind.

- Sit down, kick off your shoes, close your eyes and take a deep breath.
- Let all your thoughts just slip away.
- Imagine being wrapped in a soft, light, cashmere blanket and feeling totally supported. Take a slow deep breath and relax. Breathe in again and relax.
- Imagine being held and gently rocked, like a baby, wrapped in smooth soft cashmere.
- Feel this peace and say 'I need do nothing.'
- Take another slow, deep breath and repeat 'I need do nothing.'
- Breathe … relax … relax…
- Feel all the tension drop from your body and allow your heart to relax.
- Take another deep breath and release all your thoughts – simply let them fall away.
- Relax even more deeply into this place of safety and warmth. Feel the softest cashmere against your skin and the gentlest breeze on your face and just allow the universe to hold you.

Accessing your Miracle Mind is that easy.

Remember, for Albert Einstein, discovering that e = mc^2 was as easy as zzzzzzz …

Chapter Two

vitality

Vitality shows in not only the ability to persist but also the ability to start over.
F. SCOTT FITZGERALD

Now that you've started to listen more to your Miracle Mind, you need to seek your source of vitality. Vitality is not just about diet, exercise or a healthy body. Vitality is basically about energy. It is about having the power and ability to live life to the fullest.

Our vital force is an intangible force, a phenomenon that cannot be explained, seen or heard. We need this energy to grow and enjoy the wholeness of this lifetime. We once had vitality. We were once risk-takers and rule-breakers. We were excited about life and its possibilities. What happened? Where did the excitement go? How come our get up and go has got up and gone? In this chapter we will be looking at what drains our vital force and how we sometimes just give it away. We will look at how we can regain it and rediscover our authentic self.

☆ put the oomph back into your life!

Vitality affects every fibre and cell in your body. It gives you a spring in your step and a twinkle in your eye. It brings a richness and liveliness, so that every day becomes a celebration. It puts the oomph into your life! You start to fire on all eight cylinders rather than just ticking over. You are revitalized.

Vitality cannot be bought or bartered for. It is a natural state. It is another gift that everyone carries in their Spiritual Backpack – but often we forget it is there.

To regain our vitality and have a healthy mind and body we need to feed, nurture and most of all understand ourselves. But this can be fun; it can be easy. You will soon be laughing at yourself and your silly old ways. And once you can laugh at yourself you are free.

Angels fly because they take themselves lightly.
ANON

Once you understand more about vitality and its source, you can pass the gift on to your nearest and dearest. They may be in need of a vitality transfusion. They may be feeling low and depressed. Zap them with your newfound energy and put a smile back on their faces!

Before my High-Heeled Healer days, I would judge and blame others around me for my circumstances. In doing so I gave my power away. I didn't understand that blaming is a massive vitality drain. I used to feel as though I had a great big black hole in my stomach, an empty space that had been drained of all my energy. It is very hard to feel healthy and vibrant when you feel as if you are caving in. I felt like a burntout shadow of myself. I didn't understand that the choices I had been making had left me feeling like a victim. In fact, I had unconsciously been playing the roles of both victim and vampire – surreptitiously slurping the vitality of those around me... Oops! That was a big mistake. I now choose to act differently. Remember how important choice is – it protects you and keeps you open to greater possibilities. Ruts and routines only leave you exhausted.

Your source of energy may be wrapped in a riddle or cloaked in a conundrum – sometimes you just can't find it at all. Your vitality can feel as though it is constantly draining away and sometimes even being sucked out of you. This is why I use the term 'vampired'. Just understanding all the different ways you allow your vitality to seep away can help unwrap the riddle once and for all, thereby regaining your power and restoring your health to the optimum.

In my years as a High-Heeled Healer I have come across many examples of people who have lost their essential vitality:

Suzanne, a partner in a life-coaching company, sits at her desk staring at the stacks of paper. For weeks she hasn't been able to concentrate on her work. Her once infectious enthusiasm has deteriorated to apathy. It happens to us all, even a life coach.

Tina, a top networking agent, overhears one of her down-line team complain: 'What's the matter with Tina? She has no patience anymore and criticizes everything we do.' Tina starts to feel emotional, cries silently inside and pops another tranquillizer to dull her feelings.

Joanna, the manager of a high-street store, drags herself out of bed to go to work. 'I used to love my job,' she tells her partner, 'but now it feels unimportant. I need to do something more.'

Do any of these women's stories sound familiar? Loss of vitality is your body's reaction to the demands and pressures of the day. Stress occurs when your body reacts to anything and everything as if it was being physically threatened, so it prepares for action. You may simply be nervous about an interview or a business meeting, but your body's alarm system may be firing as intensely as if you were being attacked by a scorpion. Stress overload poses a threat to your relationship, family, health and career. The good news is that you can learn to recognize where your vitality is seeping away and take steps to stop any feelings of burnout before they undermine your goals.

Take my quick vitality test:

- Do you often feel tired or burntout?
- Do you ever feel that you can't see the point in going on?
- Are you often bored?
- Do you often feel heavy in body, mind or spirit?
- Do you feel you're living a beige kind of life?
- Do you ever feel toxic?
- Is your home in chaos?
- Are many of your relationships not working?
- How many people are you frightened of bumping into because of unfinished business?

These are all warning signals that indicate you're losing your vitality. If three or more of the questions give you concern, you are in desperate need of a vitality transfusion.

If the 'V' for vitality is missing, we end up with lies not lives. We become mere shadows of our true selves.
A.M. WOODALL

☆ meet the vitality vampires

The top three energy thieves or 'vitality vampires' are:

- ✶ Clutter buts – the time suckers
- ✶ Tolerations – the irritations and little things that bug us in the night
- ✶ Roles – the faces and masks we show the world.

These should be on the CIA, Interpol and MI5's 'Most Wanted' list. They slither around the world unnoticed, silently feeding. They are everywhere, from inner cities to the quiet rural countryside, creeping over vast continents and oceans. Nobody is safe from them. It is time for radical change, so hang on to your hat as we delve deeper into the murky world of vampires and vitality leaks.

Do you remember watching old horror films where the beautiful innocent-looking young girl walks across the room wearing a pure white dress to give the desirable young man a kiss? He is so full of expectation. Yet within seconds, instead of a big passionate kiss she is snuggling into his neck, sinking a set of sharp pointed fangs into his jugular vein. His life force is being taken and at first he doesn't even notice.

It is exactly the same with our vitality vampires when their seemingly innocent little requests start to drain our energy. At first the problems or issues seem quite small, but within a short time we become tired, unenthusiastic, listless and feel like giving up. We need larger and larger doses of adrenaline to kick-start our day. The young man thought the virginal young vamp was going to love him. He was very willing, vulnerable and innocent. What actually happened was that he became her late-night snack. He started to live a half life, walking around like a zombie, constantly in need of a fresh vitality supply. We're the same once the vitality vampires get a hold.

vitality vampire 1: the 'clutter buts'

First on our 'Most Unwanted' vamp scale are the clutter buts. Clutter is a time-sucker – the time spent looking for a telephone number or an important address because your office, home or car is cluttered takes energy away from you. Every moment spent sorting through stacks of bills, old filofaxes or handbags or looking for important information on the back of envelopes is draining your vitality.

Similarly, if your wardrobe is bursting at the seams with clothes you will never wear again there is no room for the new clothes that reflect the new you. We spend precious time sorting through old clothes, reinforcing shattered dreams of sylph-like bodies or supermodel legs. Dealing with clutter is also a good time to get real about your body and relax. Maybe you will never be a size 10 again, and even if you are, if you hang on to clothes for too long they will be dated. What is the point of giving energy to that white trouser suit that looked great when you were 20 years old? Make room for clothes that you can at least zip up, that won't split the minute you try to get into a car or step onto a bus and that reflect the real you.

Clutter demands your time. It has to be dusted, filed, or otherwise dealt with. You may use it as a distraction. But it is in the way. Mental clutter takes up space in your head; emotional clutter takes up space in your heart. It cramps and restricts you. It sucks you dry. Toss it, sell it, donate it, recycle it – just get rid of it as soon as possible.

chaos – 'can't have anyone over syndrome'

Imagine a room in your house that needs decluttering. Is it full of old newspapers, magazines, dried flowers, peeling paintwork, burnt-out candles – in fact, anything that no longer serves a purpose? Do you feel exhausted at the very thought of it? Do you simply want to close the door on it? Now think about how much energy you lost just *thinking* about that room.

Now imagine looking into that room again, only this time with the clutter completely cleared. Is there space to invite your friends over? Does it feel comfortable? Do you feel it is part of your home again? Now feel the difference in your energy level.

Over time, I have realized that my own successes frequently go hand in hand with how much clutter is invading my space. One tip in particular has served me well. Whenever I bring anything new into my space, I take at least one old thing out as soon as possible and bin it or donate it – anything, just as long as I move it out of the house as soon as possible.

When I started to clean up my act after my Shirley Valentine crisis I set myself three simple daily tasks:

- ★ Make your bed as soon as you get up
- ★ Always shower and dress for the day (no tracksuit bottoms or leggings)
- ★ Keep the kitchen sink clean and clear.

These simple rules helped me get to start the day on the right foot. It's so easy when you are getting over a relationship or feeling down to let the little things slide. My sisters could not believe I was so happy about a shiny clean sink. Actually, I was surprised at myself. But I was just getting my priorities in order.

Here's a little exercise you can do now.

- ▦ Wherever you are, either pick up your handbag or turn out your pockets.
- ▦ Take five minutes and toss out those old tissues, that one sweet with fluff and stray hairs sticking to it, those old receipts that you will never file, that business card that you once thought was vital to your future well-being, that holiday memento, that pebble or shell that was so beautiful on the beach but is now sand-covered clutter in the corner of your bag or pocket. Go on, you can do it!
- ▦ How does it feel?
- ▦ Does your handbag reflect your life?
- ▦ Just how much does that thing weigh anyhow? Is it hurting your shoulder to carry it? It may be time to change to a smaller bag.

When I started on my healing path, one of my clutter buts was my fridge. It was *cluttered* – full of outdated food producing an evolutionary chain: spoilt milk looked like yoghurt, yoghurt looked like cottage cheese, cottage cheese looked like mature cheese, which then became a perfect culture medium for my infamous penicillin-riddled blue cheese ... I really wasn't nurturing myself too well. *But* I just didn't have the time to clear it. Eventually I realized that this mode of living was not in my best interest, so I made time to sort it out and soon decluttering my fridge became a regular routine.

the 'but' stops here

So much for the *clutter*, now it's time to tackle the *buts*. Already I can hear you saying:

* ✴ '*But* I haven't got time.' What a lame excuse – I bet you've got time to watch one of the soaps on television! Remember you can *choose* the best way to spend your precious time.
* ✴ '*But* I can't throw this away, it cost me a small fortune.' OK, perhaps that's true, but now the item has served its purpose. Think of it as a transitory pleasure, like a day out on the beach or a picnic. You've had your good times with it. Now pass it on.
* ✴ '*But* I might need it someday.' Yes, that's also true and you have been cluttering yourself up for years with something you could buy again in a different size and maybe a better colour. And those sparkling Abba hot pants with matching tank top certainly won't ever come back in vogue, so let them go.
* ✴ '*But* I'm so used to it.' When you were a child you may have owned a special cuddly toy or a blanket that made you feel secure. Clutter can have the same familiar feeling, but in fact you're really just confusing clutter with comfort. It is a vitality leak, one that can be easily plugged. *It's time to let it all go.*

Start to listen to how many sentences in your life start with 'but'. A but precedes an excuse; it means you're thinking of only half changing. Buts stop you doing things. Buts negate the previous sentence. They always sound sensible and reasonable. *But* you've probably spent years producing believable excuses. List some of the excuses you use. You know what they are and doubtless they have served you well. Now it's time to get real and stop hiding behind them. The bottom line is that your buts are vamping you. They are barriers holding you back from change and success.

try the 'double but'

This is a simple technique which you can begin using straight away to weaken all those buts which are slowing your vitality and *joie de vivre*. All you need to do is listen to your thoughts and words. Look out for those buts. Some will be just feelings rather than words. However, when you look at those feelings you'll find that they are really unspoken buts.

When you think of doing something new, do you feel tired or even exhausted just at the thought of it? Or do you find you've automatically gone straight to the biscuit barrel, poured a glass of red wine or turned on the TV (a great distraction)? This is a sign there's a but lurking somewhere, sapping your vital life force. It's the Ego Dramatist's way of holding you back. However, the Miracle Mind, your friend and companion, can help you change these old negative buts into positive buts just by adding a double but. For instance, you think:

★ 'I'd like to start my diet/clean my car/answer all my messages now *but* I'm not over that tummy bug yet.'

What you need to do is immediately add, in your head or out loud, a second *but*:

★ '*But* I know I'll feel better when I've started doing something positive.'

Your double buts can be surprisingly effective:

★ ' …*but* I'm too old to start a new life, *BUT* that's daft because I've seen many people older than me change.'

* ' ...*but* I'm never going to be good enough, *BUT* then again I enjoy a challenge.'
* ' ...*but* I'm no good at sports, *BUT* I like to participate in a team so I'll give it a try.'
* ' ...*but* they told me I was no good at school, *BUT* I know better now so I'll enrol at night school.'
* ' ...*but* I'm feeling too tired to get started, *BUT* I always feel so much better when it's all been done.'

As each negative but comes up, fight back with a positive one. As soon as you rebut your buts, your fear-driven Ego Dramatist will throw another one at you. It becomes a constant battle, *but* this is the one you can always win. You can reclaim your energy, knowing that the final *but* is on your side. Something as simple as this really can affect the way you feel.

Alicia, an Australian acupuncturist, was becoming increasingly depressed about her workload. She had been very successful when she opened her practice but now it was becoming increasingly difficult for her to keep up with the demanding schedule of clients and paperwork. She had lost her energy completely. Everything seemed to be getting on top of her.

During the session I noticed her lacklustre eyes and the amount of times she made excuses for not getting some help or employing an assistant to take over the paperwork for an hour a week. Buts were flying everywhere in her vocabulary. I also learned that she watched three to four hours of television a night. Alicia saw this as her 'down time', her time to be alone and to unwind. I suggested that the time in front of the television was counterproductive. She needed to cut her viewing right down if not completely out. Alicia had a whole range of buts ready in protest:

* 'But I need to escape from work and it's how I stop thinking about it.'
* 'But I'll miss all the soaps ...'
* 'But it's the only way I can relax.'

In fact, vegging out in front of 'the box' is a stimulant and was probably one of the reasons why Alicia wasn't sleeping. She said cutting down her viewing would be a stretch *but* she would try. She left with three homework tasks for the first week:

☆ She was to be in bed by 10 p.m. to allow her body to become naturally revitalized.

☆ She was to clean out just one set of drawers, discarding anything she hadn't used for more than a year.

☆ She was to start to list her buts and old worn-out excuses and then try to find double buts to negate them.

After a week, Alicia felt much better. Although tough at first, the curfew helped enormously, as did cutting out the television. Her biggest surprise, however, was her list of excuses. These overwhelmed her when she realized how pathetic they must have sounded to everyone in her life. Emptying the drawers was also absolutely invigorating. She had found tights and bras that were older than her daughter, who was now ten years old, and to boot the charity shop staff were pleased to receive her tank tops, flowery hippie skirts (size eight) and unused Green Goddess lycra workout gear. As the weeks passed it became easier to be ruthless in dealing with the creeping clutter that had taken over her life. Alicia and several of her friends threatened to create 'Clutter Anon', a 12-step programme for the befuddled, untidy and chaotic.

vitality vampire 2: tolerations

The second major vitality vampires are tolerations. Tolerations are things that we put up with in life. A fair chunk of our vitality may be held hostage by them. They may be minor, but minor irritations, like small streams, accumulate to create large rivers of annoyance.

Tolerations remind me of Jonathan Swift's *Gulliver's Travels* when Gulliver wakes up in Lilliput to find himself tied down by hundreds of little things. Fine ropes and straps incapacitate him totally. Individually, none could have held him, but hundreds of ties combine to prevent him from moving. Tolerations do the same. The inertia we feel is a product of the fear-driven Ego Dramatist – it is a trap frightening us into total paralysis.

We tolerate because when we were younger we learned to 'keep the peace' or 'not rock the boat' and now we are used to saying things like 'Oh, that's OK' or 'It doesn't really matter' or 'It's not worth complaining about.' We believe that we just have to put up with a certain amount of 'stuff'. This is *not true*!

Tolerations chip away at your confidence, hopefulness and enthusiasm. They drag you down, making you feel lethargic. Tolerations are unbelievable energy thieves. They come in many guises: broken zips; loose and missing buttons; defunct office equipment; lank, dull hair; too much fat and unhealthy food which adds to the flab already deposited around a once vital healthy skeleton; a chaotic home; a dead-end job, payment demands from the telephone, gas and electricity suppliers, late and missed credit-card payments... How many times have you said 'I must do something about that'? You may try to ignore it – but deliberately not paying attention to something takes just as much energy as being fully aware of it.

Of course, people can also be energy thieves – these are the people who catch you at inopportune moments and hone straight in on your vitality jugular. They criticize, they moan, they want to have a pity party for at least an hour per week. You listen to their miseries and they demand your time and space. They drink your vitality. Energy thieves don't want you to change, they liked the old you. These people feed off friends and family, in fact they will feed off anyone who stops to listen or to help. Energy thieves aren't bad, they just aren't ready to be accountable for their lives. When you step onto the path of transformation, you will start to be more discerning about whom you spend your time with. Sometimes you may falter, but one thing is for sure: you will never go back to playing small again.

Start listing your tolerations:

- ▪ List five to ten tolerations from your home.
- ▪ List ten tolerations from your workplace.
- ▪ List ten tolerations from your relationships.
- ▪ List ten tolerations from your lifestyle.
- ▪ List at least three people who have a quick slurp of your vitality.
- ▪ List three people who leave you energized.
- ▪ What do they do to make you feel good about yourself?

On a scale of one to ten, how much energy are you giving away to each of these tolerations and energy thieves? Put them in descending order and make the decision to take action now. Clear them in order of importance to you.

Many seminar participants have asked me, 'What about the tolerations you just can't change?' I reply that with the help of a little imagination and your Miracle Mind you can change anything. If you start from the position that anything can be transformed, or at least made easier, new solutions will appear. You can also reduce the psychological drain of tolerations by changing the way you see them. Remember your soul protection factor — accountability and choice can help you to protect your energy. Often simply reorganizing your life will help to keep your stress levels to a minimum and your vitality levels up…

Next it is time to turn your attention to what you are tolerating from yourself. We are often our own worst enemy. For example, are you often careless, late for appointments, always making arrangements you don't really want to keep? In relation to health issues, are you:

- ★ Tolerating missing fillings, stained teeth or inadequate prescriptions for your glasses?
- ★ Tolerating back pain and stiff joints?
- ★ Tolerating breathlessness or bad skin?

⭐ Tolerating that lingering cold or cough?

⭐ Tolerating eating or drinking too much or being on a constant diet?

What you need to stop tolerating is the endless futile struggle which is sapping your energy and happiness. Remember the accountability factor. It's *your* choice. You've chosen your tolerations. They can be changed. The way forward is to focus on positive new behaviour.

Finally, it is time to come clean about what other people may be tolerating from you. How many times have you pushed your luck by behaving a certain way – maybe sly sarcastic remarks or pushing people's buttons to hurt them – when really, on the inside, you would like someone to stop you?

Here's an exercise for your journal. Remember to be as honest as you can:

▨ How do you behave when you meet certain members of your family? What is the behaviour your mum and dad still tolerate from you? Do you act like a teenage brat even though you are nearer 40 than 14?

▨ What behaviour do colleagues at work tolerate?

▨ What about your partner – would you talk to your best friend the way you do to your partner? If you did, do you think the friend would stay around for long?

▨ What about your children, what do they tolerate from you? You would be surprised at the number of adults I meet on my travels who are still hurting from their *parents'* childish behaviour. Sometimes we worry about what our child will be tomorrow, yet forget that they are someone today.

You know when you are off track. Do any of these sound familiar?

⭐ sarcastic remarks

⭐ criticism

⭐ lateness

⭐ carelessness

⭐ thoughtlessness

Would you choose to change? To free somebody else from the toleration ties by which you bind them? Take a peek inside your Spiritual Backpack. What gift do you think would help the person you are vamping off? Could they do with a zap of recognition? A zing of acknowledgement? A kind thought? This is your chance to feel revitalized, to feel energized, to get excited about life again. Give your gifts and reap the reward of vitality.

A Canadian client, Joan, told me this salutary tale about tolerations. The first on her list had been her husband Tommy's sloppiness. He never put his clothes away; he would leave them all over the place on the bedroom floor, hung over doors, draped on a chair or rolled up in a corner of the room. He would step out of socks and underpants and leave them where they fell. Joan felt that this was driving her insane.

But when she tried to put Tommy's things in the wardrobe, she found that there was no room for them. It was cluttered with her things, some of which had not seen daylight for years. Tommy, seeing her dilemma, said that he left his clothes on the floor because he was 'tolerating' her hoarding rather than cause a fuss.

This was a valuable lesson for Joan. She and Tommy made a list of what each was tolerating for the sake of 'peace' and decided to be more open with one another. The knock-on effect of these tolerations could have led to a breakdown of communication, which is the single biggest problem in relationships. Now that Joan and Tommy have cleared up these tolerations, their decluttered boudoir is more of a passion pad than a jumble sale. Their extra vitality improved their sex life in leaps and bounds!

You don't notice how much a toleration is draining you until you've cleared it – but then it can be a revelation. Any toleration you clear has a positive knock-on effect – releasing energy, lightening your heart and making the next one you come across that much easier to tackle. Understanding this simple concept and putting it into practice will make a tremendous difference to your life.

vitality vampire 3: roles

The third and biggest energy vampires are the roles that we play. They can sap up to 90 per cent of our vital life force. We are not talking bread, breakfast or dinner rolls here – they can be fun for food groupies like me – but energy-sapping roles, ugh! We can have an entire regiment of roles: good girl/boy, victim, vampire, martyr and sacrificer, to name but a few. In later chapters we will look at the roles we all play within our families and relationships and with our work colleagues. Here we will look at some of the *core roles* we all play.

Roles are a defence, a mechanism we set up to protect ourselves, to mask our feelings of fear, loss, hurt, rejection, abandonment and guilt. Once our innocent, trusting selves have been knocked down or about by the cruel world a few times we learn to present ourselves differently to the world. We start to present a face that masks our true feelings – often to the extent of obliterating all emotion in the mistaken belief that emotion equals pain.

Our roles may have developed to protect our fragile hearts and shattered dreams, but they invariably end up distorting our true emotions. Eventually we don't even know who we are supposed to be any longer!

Roles are also massive vitality vamps. We expend huge amounts of energy trying to prove to others that we really are something we are not. Roles are the number one reason for burnout, pain, illness, stress and low spirits.

As our energy depletes we start to live on adrenaline. We have to get our kicks through an adrenaline rush from a bottle, a certain weed, having sex with strangers or becoming workaholics. Addiction takes many forms. Too much adrenaline is toxic. It will physically burn you up inside and poison everything you try to do. At this point of exhaustion businesses start to fail, relationships become rocky and everything seems to lead to more heartbreak. Inspiration eludes us. Creativity is something we just read about. Health issues start to worry us. Every little detail becomes a mountain of misery. We become mean-mouthed and frugal-faced worry warriors. The roles we play in our quest for happiness actually end up killing us.

When you play a role you're not living, you are existing, like a zombie going through the motions. You can't feel success, love and enthusiasm. You have thrown both the good and the bad feelings away. You are incomplete, weak, drained and soulless.

☆ rediscover the 'authentic' you

Man's main task in life is to give birth to himself, to become what he potentially is. The most important product of his effort is his own personality.
ERICH FROMM

When you ignore your true giftedness and instead enact roles, you become a performer rather than an authentic person. And to perform 24 hours a day, seven days a week is exhausting to say the least. Your roles may have developed in the first place for very good reasons – you may have found that it was easier to fill the roles your family and friends expected of you, rather than becoming who you really wanted to be. But now you need to pursue the things you truly value, to discover your authentic self.

The 'authentic' self is the you that can be found at your absolute core. It is the part of you not defined by your job, or function, or role. It is the composite of all your skills, talents and wisdom. It is all of the things that are uniquely yours and need expression, rather than what you believe you are supposed to be and do.
PHILIP C. MCGRAW

so which part do you play?

When you're asked 'Who are you?', what is your answer? 'I'm a teacher/mother/the wife of/live in London'? Often the answer is not who you are, but what you do or where you live or whom you are married to. You can't say who you are, because you don't know.

Do you know which roles you are playing? Do you know why you're playing them? A role is a mistaken belief about ourselves. When as a child we were told that we were lazy we might have become super-industrious in order to prove to our parent/teacher/sibling that we were not. This over-compensation can lead to the role of the workaholic. Alternatively, we might have accepted the criticism and played the role of the failure, feeling unable to live up to the expectations placed upon us. Both of these are victim roles. But when you accept that these are just roles, you can place the responsibility for life, liberty and the pursuit of happiness in your own hands, where it ultimately belongs. You can start being fully accountable to yourself again.

As I stressed earlier, when you are living a role life becomes difficult. You are unable truly to connect with anybody. You feel you are a fraud. You are afraid you will be found out and then people won't like or love or trust you. So you pretend you have everything under control. For example, you may play the role of 'the independent', telling the world 'I don't need anything from anybody. You can't hurt me. I am fine just as I am, thank you very much.' In truth the independent is not fine, but is hiding some form of heartbreak from childhood. And hiding feelings such as loss, abandonment and grief under the mask of sacrifice causes us to become depressed, disillusioned, burntout and boring.

Alternatively, another common role is that of 'the dependant'. This is a role we take on as compensation for a past loss that we have yet to come to terms with. We show the world how 'sensitive', 'emotional' or 'caring' we are and believe that we must be protected by those more able to cope with life's troubles. We want somebody to notice our long sad face, to come and save us. God! Why would anyone want to bother?! Those kind souls who do try to help soon find that a dependant can emotionally manipulate and blackmail to Olympic gold-medal standard. But the costs are often enormous. In this role the emotions we carry feel like great tidal waves threatening to overwhelm us with sadness and despair, and it takes vast amounts of our energy to keep this sad sack face in the first place. This role not only vamps others, but even sillier, it vamps our own energy.

Dependants can vampire easily for a short time. Then people start to notice that all they are doing is taking. They may feel happy momentarily after a quick slurp, but then it's back to the emotional swamp. 'Feed me, feed me! Tell me you love me!' says the Swamp King or Queen. 'Show me you care!' Dependants set up tests for people, mini SAS assault courses such as:

* ⋆ 'If you love me, swim across the toxic lake of my tears.'
* ⋆ 'If you love me, jump through the fiery hoops of my temper.'
* ⋆ 'If you love me, crawl on your belly through the broken shards of my dreams.'
* ⋆ 'If you love me, give up your life and come and join me on the cross …'

'What? You must be joking!' I have heard many a hero shout as he packed his bags and left. There are many different tests we set. What are yours?

get off the cross, we need the wood!

You are not capable of being tired, but you are very capable of wearying yourself. The strain of constant judgment is virtually intolerable.
A COURSE IN MIRACLES

Another common role is 'the sacrificer'. Have you ever felt like a sacrificial lamb? That no matter what you do or say, you are always in the wrong? At this point many people decide to lie down and become a doormat or a dormouse, though nobody would know it, because the message they give the world is 'Everything is alright. I am a good person.'

The role of sacrificer is usually based on a childhood belief that we had to save the family. Unable to fulfil this impossible goal, we feel unworthy and guilty and in response go into service mode to prove that we are competent and loveable. We help everybody, but this is an act of avoidance, an attempt not to feel our own anger and pain. Think for a minute of somebody in your life who is always available and seemingly willing to organize the school fête or the staff party, or campaigning to save the rainforest, or the whales, or the planet, not to mention the myriad other committees they are on. Could this be you?

Sacrificers believe that if you want a job done properly you have to do it yourself, otherwise you will be let down. They often feel disappointed. The silly thing is that although initially we sacrifice out of love, if we keep playing this role we will be disappointed, either in others or in ourselves. We can never receive an equal partner because we would either put the person above us and feel inferior to them, or put them below us and then feel superior. Neither of these is a win/win scenario.

I've only described the three core roles people play; of course there are endless variations of these. But there is hope. Forget all the roles – this is the time to choose to become authentic and to start being accountable for the way your life has been so far.

The first step away from dependency on roles is to be honest about your behaviour.

- In your journal make a list of all the different roles you play in your life.
- Then think about how much energy you are losing by acting out each of these roles.
- Using your intuitive mind (or just guessing), pick a number from 1 to 100 to see which roles are draining you the most. As you start to let your intuition help you it will feel as though you are stepping from your shell. This could be the first step in using your psychic ability!

Once you are honest about your behaviour, the next step is to discover what your needs are and to find ways to fulfil them for yourself. You can do it – you are totally gifted and whole just as you are. In your Spiritual Backpack you have everything you need to find purpose, passion and adventure. All you have to do is to start looking up, waking up and sharing those gifts.

For example, if you want to be loved, choose to give love and then you are free. If you want respect, choose to give respect. If you want friendship, choose to be a good friend. Next time you feel as though you are being swamped by your emotions, ask: 'Who needs my help?' You don't have to physically go and help them – all you have to do is be aware that you are here to learn lessons. The Miracle Mind will help you by giving you signs. A sign may come as a headline in a newspaper or an advert on a bus or even a snippet of overheard conversation. Then, as you learn each lesson and decide to move on, you will see somebody around you who is in exactly the place where you were stuck before – and now you will be able to offer them the gift of help.

This is an exercise for your journal. Think about the following questions and use your intuition to guide your answers:

- When or at what age did you lose heart?
- When did you pull back from life?
- What made you decide to hide your gifts?
- What burden of disappointment are you carrying that is stealing your vitality?

Then take time to meditate on these suggestions:

- Today, could you let all the burdens and disappointments of life drop from your shoulders?
- Today, could you pick up your fragile heart and allow a friend to help you for a change?
- Today, could you ask for help from someone? (Believe me, it could save your life.)

☆ a recap of the vital points

Vitality affects every fibre of our being. It is a natural state, a gift provided in our heavenly Spiritual Backpack. Vitality is available to all of us – all we need do is ask. We are all true, innocent, gifted beings. We are more than the sum of the many roles that we play. Our roles are merely a façade, they hide our authentic self. With accountability as the healing principle we can remember the choices we made to play them. We can also make new choices. We may have many shattered dreams, but it is never too late to have another dream. It is possible to replace the pain with a new vision.

If one advances confidently in the direction of his dreams, and endeavours to live the life which he has imagined, he will meet with a success unexpected in common hours.

HENRY DAVID THOREAU

☆ healerette's happy hour

This 'Act As If' exercise is all about discarding old roles and trying new ones for fun. Playact for a day, or at least for an hour, just to get it out of your system.

* If you could be anyone in the world, who would it be? A good or a bad character? What would you wear? What would you eat? How would you speak?
* Would you be a heroine from times gone by? Joan of Arc? Watch out for those flames!
* Or a head of state? If it's Gandhi you could wear a sheet for an hour …

* Or how about the Iron Lady herself, Margaret Thatcher? Just carry a handbag and walk with an air of authority.
* How about a film star? Be Audrey Hepburn – become very demure, extend your vowels and wear a long pair of gloves (even rubber gloves would do!) and a string of pearls. Or maybe you prefer Catherine Zeta Jones and will talk with a soft Welsh accent for the day.
* If sexy singers are more your thing, have fun making a tape for different moods. Try singing in the style of J-Lo, Shania Twain or Dolly Parton, all to the same piece of music. How would Dolly's *D.I.V.O.R.C.E.* sound sung in the style of Madonna?
* Does the idea of being a superhuman cartoon character like Lara Croft or Wonder Woman appeal?
* Invite a few friends over and go the whole hog. Have a fancy-dress party, hamming your role up as much as you want.

The point of this exercise is to get out of your rut and see the world from a new perspective. And this kind of conscious role-play can be fun. When you've finished your role-play for the day, acknowledge your courage and your ability to be a 'secret agent of change' … and maybe don't tell anyone!

Chapter Three

happiness

Places and circumstances never guarantee happiness. You must decide within yourself whether you want to be happy. And once you've decided, happiness comes much easier.
ROBERT J. HASTINGS

Every person in the whole world is in search of happiness. For the Buddhist it is the quest for Nirvana, for the romantic it is the perfect relationship, for an increasing number of people it is the body beautiful. For the workaholic, it's work. Happiness comes in many disguises. We search for it everywhere. Intrepid travellers go to the highest, lowest, hottest, coldest, most hidden places on earth in search of their dream destination where happiness may be waiting. Drugs can promise happiness, but you will reach the perfect high only to find the lows are deeper than imaginable. Or how about a celebration drink? You're bound to be happy then – until the hangover.

There is a Hungarian proverb: 'When ambition ends, happiness begins.' Think about it – is your ambition to achieve happiness actually preventing you from finding it? In this chapter we will see how happiness often lies as much in the journey as in the arrival. We will also remember that happiness is one of the gifts we brought with us in our Spiritual Backpack. *Happiness is a state of mind and a state of heart. Most of all it is a gift.*

I believe that happiness is about being in love with living 100 per cent. It is based on what you value in your life. It is based on what you value in yourself. Happiness is more than mere possessions or even reaching your goals. It is more than transitory pleasures that only last for a few moments. It's an inner knowing and a connection to All That Is True; it is where you feel supported and loved; it is the peace of mind in which you are able to find the authentic self.

As I have said, happiness is a gift; as with vitality, it cannot be bought or sold. The paradox is that in order to receive the gift, we must first be prepared to give it. But how can you give something that you don't know you have? The truth is that your Miracle Mind is shouting loud and clear for you to remember you *do* have it all, just look into your Backpack. If there is a problem, it is that the pack has become hidden under layers and layers of beliefs, roles, disappointment and criticism. These hidden beliefs become blocks to finding purpose, passion and adventure. They help create the racket we use to push people away. This then leaves us feeling sad, separate and lonely. Not a good place to be.

The Ego Dramatist needs us to hold on to our racket because it has the mistaken belief that it is protecting us from further hurt in the form of disappointment, expectation, competition and criticism. But as with gifts, so with criticism and competition – you get what you give. If you compete, criticize or have expectations of a person or situation, you will undoubtedly be disappointed. These are, as we will see later, major blocks to happiness.

Imagine a world where there is no competition, where criticism and disappointment do not exist. This is not some Utopian dream – it can be achieved. It can be *your* world.

☆ it's not just about scoring goals

This brings us back to what happiness means to you. Is it achieving your goals? Perfect health? Winning the lottery?

Do you find yourself thinking, 'I'll be happy when …'

* ★ 'I've lost 10/20/30 pounds in weight.'
* ★ 'I leave home/buy a new house.'
* ★ 'I get my degree/new job/promotion.'
* ★ 'I have enough money to pay off my debts/go to Barbados.'
* ★ 'I meet Mr/Miss Perfect.'

In my pre-Healerette days I would have said at this point, 'I will be happy when this book is finished.' What I now know is that happiness is not really about this. How many times have you felt that the anticipation is far better than the event? Do you remember as a teenager getting ready to go into town for a night out with the girls? It was great fun choosing what to wear and which clubs we would visit, and most important of all, wondering what boys we would meet. We believed that meeting that dream guy with the dream body and the dream car would take us on a dream boat to happiness. Did you do the same? How many times did you go home disappointed, not appreciating that the real happiness was being in the moment with your friends? This is what we do in our lives – we spend our time looking to the future or reminiscing on the past. This makes it impossible for us to be happy in the moment.

Similarly, if you believe that happiness is the attainment of a goal such as getting that new car, house or promotion, then what? Once you've achieved one goal, you have to create the next. You will never be satisfied. It's a constant treadmill.

A Spanish client had set herself the goal of owning a convertible sports car by the time she was 30. On her thirtieth birthday, the car was duly delivered, wrapped in a big red ribbon. She was so happy she cried. The euphoria lasted for a whole five minutes. As she sat in the car she asked her husband to take a photograph of her in it. He was surprised and asked, 'Don't you want to drive it first and feel the power?' 'No,' she replied. 'It looks so much more fun from the outside.'

This tale shows what an illusion happiness can be – especially when our Ego Dramatist tricks us into thinking happiness lies in an object or a relationship, that happiness is an 'outside job'.

☆ happiness is an 'inside job'

The person who knows how to laugh at himself will never cease to be amused.
SHIRLEY MACLAINE

Can you remember the last time you were happy? I mean really happy. When you felt content and the world seemed to be a safe place. What were you doing? I bet any money it was something simple. Could it have been watching the first snowflakes falling in winter? Or was it the wonder of an intricate spider's web in the early spring morning with dew still shimmering in the faint sunlight? Maybe it was enjoying a perfect sunset on the last days of your summer break.

A few years ago, a few days before Christmas, I'd finished work for the year and cleaned the house from top to bottom. There was fresh food in the fridge, the bills had all been paid on time and I'd had a great time clearing all the clutter from my office. I felt as though the house was gleaming; even the fruit in the bowl looked shiny. Woody, my guy, had finished work early and surprised me with a lovely bottle of champagne, which he opened as I lit the log fire. As we sat down together I felt an overwhelming feeling of ease, peace, trust and love. Was this the fabled feeling of happiness?

In my 'Drama Queen' days I would have had to be out somewhere or other proving how happy I was by partying till four in the morning. But I remembered going home most nights and not feeling that happy; in fact I felt sad. Not that I would have let anybody know.

The phone rang. It was a friend wishing me a happy Christmas. 'How are you doing?' she asked. I replied, 'Well, I am embarrassed to say I feel really content.' It was the simplicity of just being in that moment that brought me, albeit briefly, that sense of contentment.

These unexpected moments of happiness are just that – moments. We should savour them and then let them go. If we try to recreate a moment we will place an expectation on the outcome. Expectation is one of the main blocks to happiness.

My life has no purpose, no direction, no aim, no meaning, and yet I'm happy. I can't figure it out. What am I doing right?
CHARLES M. SCHULZ

☆ major blocks to happiness: your hidden beliefs

There are a number of blocks to achieving happiness. In my experience the two most common are our hidden beliefs, where our thoughts are stuck in a time warp, and our family histories.

To be truly happy requires knowledge about your beliefs. Beliefs are fixed thoughts from the past; they colour our experiences, which in turn create our world. They may be conscious or subconscious thoughts and they can come from both positive and negative situations. But when they get stuck in a time warp, they restrict our ability to be happy.

Just knowing which of your beliefs are making you happy or unhappy can help you take the first step on a happier journey.

Happy Beliefs	Unhappy Beliefs
★ 'There is a meaning to life.'	'Life has no meaning.'
★ 'Earth is a schoolroom.'	'There is no reason for life's events.'
★ 'There is no blame.'	'It is all their fault.'
★ 'I get exactly what I need.'	'I am a victim.'
★ 'This is a safe world.'	'This world is unsafe.'

Delia, a 40-year-old lady, came to see me. She complained that she felt continually rejected. We did a number of exercises around her hidden belief systems to find out what was really going on. Remember that beliefs are merely thoughts that got stuck in time.

It transpired that when Delia was four years old her mum had had to go into hospital. Children were not allowed to visit. Nobody thought to explain to Delia that this was a hospital rule. Delia believed that her mother had abandoned and rejected her. This was totally unfounded. But in her four-year-old black-and-white mind, Delia came to the conclusion: 'My mum doesn't want me.' Delia never discussed this with her mum – she buried the thought and it became stuck in a time warp.

That hidden belief had affected Delia's perception of herself and of her relationships. She subconsciously believed that if her mother didn't want her how could anyone else? The seemingly minor incident had restricted her ability to be happy. It was only after we had explored her beliefs in some depth that the real cause of her fear was uncovered.

Are you running your life on silly trapped thoughts?

i'll be happy when ...

We all think we know what will make us happy. How many times have you said 'I will be happy when …'? I did this exercise with a group recently.

Mary wrote, 'I will be happy when I lose 20 pounds and am down to dress size 12.' What she didn't realize was that behind her answer there was a hidden belief that achieving the goal would not really make her happy.

Let us look at what was hidden behind Mary's answer. I asked her to list why she *didn't* want to lose weight. She thought for a while and surprised herself with her answers:

* 'Because it's too hard.'
* 'Because I'll only put it all back on again.'
* 'Because I always fail.'
* 'By keeping this size my husband is proving to me he loves me no matter what size I am.'

On the surface Mary was saying losing 20 pounds would make her happy, yet her hidden beliefs were actually saying something entirely different.

Another client, Peter, answered, 'I'll be happy when I've got my degree.' Again, I asked Peter to write down four hidden beliefs about what might happen after he had attained his degree. These were his answers:

* 'I will miss the fun and freedom of university life.'
* 'I will have to compete with other graduates in the job stakes.'
* 'I will be a little fish in a big pond.'
* 'I'll have student debts for years.'

In Peter's case not only will the goal of the degree not bring sustained happiness, but the journey is proving to be more fun. As I explained earlier, this is an important point about happiness. Often the journey is where the happiness is, not the destination. We could choose to enjoy exactly where we are now – and in Peter's case just acknowledging this ambivalence helped him to overcome it and move on to the next stage in his life.

Discovering your own hidden beliefs is the key to unleashing happiness into your life. What hidden beliefs do you have?

Try this simple exercise – you may surprise yourself. Use your journal to write down the first thing that comes into your mind. Allow your Miracle Mind to give you some help:

- Happiness is …
- Unhappiness is …
- I can't be happy because …

Every time I finish a seminar I am amazed at the pain we seemingly happy successful people are carrying around with us. These are some of the answers I've seen in my seminars:

- Happiness is … short term.
- Happiness is … having a perfect partner.
- Happiness is … a big chocolate cake.
- Happiness is … love.
- Happiness is … a happy family.

- Unhappiness is … being alone.
- Unhappiness is … being poor.
- Unhappiness is … being with the wrong partner.
- Unhappiness is … family rifts.
- Unhappiness is … feeling unloved.

Old stuck beliefs like this create internal clutter, which blocks the flow of happiness. The good news is that I have watched participants transform their lives by using the gifts of choice and understanding to change their mistaken beliefs.

As we progress in life we all need to clear up our internal clutter. Let's do an inventory of where you are at present on the happiness scale. I call this the 'Happyometer'. Mine could go something like this:

I saw a beautiful sunset which registered at seven on my happiness scale. The next moment I may have had an expectation that wasn't fulfilled and felt disappointed, reducing my score to two.

It is possible to have many emotions running at the same time. You may flick from happy to unhappy and back again. It is your choice which of these you decide to focus upon.

Try asking yourself some of these questions each day. They will help you focus on the best things in your life, whether they are your family, work, home or recreation.

- What am I most happy about in my life now?
- What is it about this that makes me feel happy?
- What am I excited about in my life now?
- What am I proud of in my life now?
- What am I grateful for in my life now?
- Whom would I like to thank?
- What did I dream of being as a child?

Keeping a Happyometer will also show you what you value in your daily life.

know your values

It has been said that to be happy you must discover what makes your heart miss a beat. It's a signpost from the universe as to what your purpose is. As your path unfolds and you start to follow your life's purpose, you will become happy. Time disappears and eternity begins. You have made the connection back to heaven.

The most wasted of all days is one without laughter.
E. E. CUMMINGS

a crisis is also an opportunity

The swing between emotions and the decision to focus upon happiness was brought home to me most poignantly by the terrible tragedy in New York on 11 September 2001. This stopped me in my tracks; I thought my life was set, I thought I knew where I was and where I was going; I believed I knew what made me happy. But watching this tragedy live on TV made me, and probably millions of others, reassess my life path. I felt shocked, scared, confused and in a state of high anxiety. I telephoned my children, my parents and all of my brothers and sisters. I felt an urgent need to reconnect with my immediate family members, to reassure and to be reassured. That night I prayed for those who had lost their loved ones in the Twin Towers. I also prayed for the souls of those who had died.

The next day, after much soul-searching about my life, I walked along the deserted beach near my home. I walked for 15 minutes. Walking made me feel better, watching the clouds, feeling the breeze and smelling the ocean and tasting the sea air. I realized that even amongst the chaos that was the world I could still find brief moments of happiness. I asked myself: 'What would make me happy now?' To my surprise, it was to eat a full English breakfast. I went to a café and spent 15 minutes eating breakfast, which made me happy. I then asked myself again, 'What would make me happy now?' I decided it was to cook and share a wholesome meal full of goodness, made with love. I walked to the supermarket and carefully chose each ingredient for its colour, texture and taste. I noticed the goodness of each item down to its minutest detail. Choosing the ingredients took a further 15 minutes, in which I felt happy. I took my purchases home and phoned some friends, inviting them over for dinner. As I cooked the meal I realized that the whole day I had been asking myself what would make me happy now. I had reinforced the choice to be happy at regular 15-minute intervals. What this episode showed me was that sustained happiness can only be achieved through making a conscious choice here and now. To remain happy we must reinforce that choice at regular intervals.

In Chinese, the word for 'crisis' is the same as for 'opportunity'. Walking on the beach, I took the opportunity to evaluate my happiness. First, I looked at my relationships. I evaluated who added to my vitality and who drew from it. I realized it was time to let go of certain people emotionally and to complete with others. I made a pact with myself to clear these areas of my life within two weeks of the attacks, and I succeeded. As a result, I had less stress and more time to concentrate on the relationships that mattered most to me.

make gratitude your attitude

Gratitude is one of the very best ways to instant happiness. You cannot be unhappy if you are feeling grateful. Make a list of all the things you are grateful for. Then start doing these things right now:

* Thank your friends for their support.
* Acknowledge all the love you have been given by your spouse.
* Tell your children and family you love them.
* Think about all the small things you are grateful for.
* Just keep focusing on nature around you – the wonder of a sunrise, the beauty of a sunset.

☆ major blocks to happiness: your family history

Ninety per cent of the work I do is based on the healing of relationships within the family, the reason being that families are usually the main source of our conditioning, which impacts upon our beliefs about happiness. These old stuck thoughts create internal clutter, which blocks the flow of happiness. My first reaction on watching the September disaster was *not* to check what money I had left in the bank or what my house was worth or for that matter anything to do with outside effects: it didn't matter if the house needed cleaning. Although there have been many times in my life when I have tried to run away from my family and even pretend that they didn't matter, my instinct, and that of millions of others around the world, was to ring my family.

On my epic Shirley Valentine Ego Drama it didn't take me long to realize that you can't leave your family. When I was sitting on my big cerise towel on that exotic beach, having run thousands of miles away from home, it didn't stop me thinking of what had happened in my family as a child. My family was in my head – that towel was extremely crowded! The expectations, disappointments, criticism and competition from within your family can follow you through your life like little energy thieves, stealing your happiness. Of course this is not the fault of the family, it's your Ego Dramatist using your mistaken beliefs and judgements to stop you from being happy

What is your idea of a happy family? Is it the Waltons, the fictional television family who live in Midwest America on a great ranch, staying together and being totally supportive of each other? Or is it the Larkin family in H. E. Bates' *The Darling Buds of May* – lots of drama but it all comes right in the end? Is it a family where nobody ever argues? Or is it a family where you can always say what you want? Is it the perfect home with food on the table and logs in the fire? Is it a place of safety where you can feel valued and acknowledged? Take some time now to describe in your journal your idea of a perfect family.

family roles

Yes, we're back with the roles we all play again, only here we're looking at them purely from within the family. Everything that goes on in our family leaves an indelible impression on our beliefs, our values and expectations. As children, we pick up on every emotion: success, failure, happiness, sadness, jubilation, joy, guilt and loss. We construct intricate barricades to protect ourselves from the painful emotions while simultaneously longing to be able to help. This inner conflict leads to the production of a regiment of roles. As we learnt earlier, these roles hold us hostage to outdated beliefs long into adulthood.

Our Ego Dramatist has a field day with family roles; that's why there are so many tears and tantrums. The unhealed criticism and disappointment from our family help to keep the rackets going. Next we will clear up some of those old misunderstandings so we are able to give and receive more happiness.

criticism

When we are children the first place we hear and receive criticism is within the family. Here the rackets aren't even hidden, we are all fair game and we whack, wallop and thwack each other mercilessly.

What does criticism achieve? It certainly doesn't make you more likeable. The reason people criticize is the same reason why people rule by fear: they feel unlovable and afraid.

Take some time to think about how much time you spend criticizing others.

- Who are you still criticizing in your family?
- What are you criticizing them for?
- Can you see that maybe these criticisms are a projection of things you find unacceptable about yourself?

disappointments

It is not only family members that press our buttons. We often sabotage our own happiness by setting ourselves up for disappointment. Have you ever been disappointed in yourself? Many of us say or do things that we later regret. Usually we experience the embarrassment and get on with our lives. But sometimes we do or say things that we believe are beyond forgetting. These become embedded in our self-belief system, setting us up for a lifetime of disappointment.

Again, take some time to think about these questions:

- When did you first feel disappointed in yourself?
- Who in your family disappointed you?
- When was the last time you felt you disappointed somebody?
- Can you forgive yourself and them?

expectations

All too often our expectations can never really be met. No matter how hard we try, something will not be quite right. Imagine going into a large white room that has been freshly painted and looks superb, then looking around and finding the one tiny weeny patch high up in the corner that has been missed. The negative and fearful part of your mind – the Ego Dramatist – will concentrate only on the mistake, not on the beauty of the other paintwork. That's what happens with expectations – they are never quite met. Take some time to think about unrealistic expectations you are carrying around that are blocking your chances of happiness.

Criticism, disappointment and unfulfilled expectations are often where family role-playing begins. We assume we have let down both ourselves and our family and are not worthy of them. Alternatively, we project this negativity onto another family member and decide that they are not worthy of the family. All these negative feelings can be healed by the gift of forgiveness.

The roles we play are also often a defence to hide our guilt, the guilt for not sharing our gifts with the family. It's time to let go of guilt. It's never too late to give those gifts.

some archetypal roles

In most families there will be several archetypal roles being played out. Here are some of the familiar ones:

the hero

The hero is the star of the family: the head girl, the high achiever, the sports star and the scholar – the one that is obviously set for success. These are the deputy mums and next-in-line dads taking charge of the vulnerable ones and managing mum and dad. As adults they are the Supermen and Wonder Women who work 60 hours a week and take care of the kids whilst keeping an eye on their parents, finishing all of the housework, organizing a street party and feeding all of their friends. The hero seeks to prove to the world that the family is doing just fine.

the trophy child

The trophy child is a role in which the mother and daughter or father and son dress alike, act like friends and go everywhere together. The trophy child becomes the surrogate partner, therapist and friend. It's the mini-me syndrome. The child is being vampired by the parent, who is taking the child's energy and using it to gain attention, playing the role of sister or brother instead of mum or dad. There are no real boundaries in this relationship and the trophy child loses their sense of identity and feels like a fraud.

the martyr

This is the child who always gets ill, falls over and gives their toys to the poor. Martyrs are caught in the Cinderella syndrome, suffering for the sake of the family. They are the wounded soldiers, the sickly child, the saints-in-the-making who'll sacrifice their health, wealth and sanity in the mistaken belief that 'If I take on the pain in the family, everyone will get along a lot better.'

the scapegoat

The scapegoat brings in outside forces such as the police and social services in an effort to get help for the family as a whole. This is the wild child, the black sheep, the bad boy, the rebel. They'll get drunk, get pregnant, shoplift, take drugs and make mischief – anything to get attention in the hope that then the family will pull together again.

the lost child

The lost child believes life would be better for everyone else if they weren't there, so they try to disappear. They are the quiet ones, the plain Janes, the shrinking Violets, the invisible men and the prodigal sons. They can disappear in a room, melt into a crowd and lose themselves in their imagination. The '*Home Alone* syndrome' is when the family doesn't realize that this one has gone missing. If all else fails, they'll emigrate.

the entertainer

Happy, happy, happy on the surface and hurt, hurt, hurt inside. Cute, funny and foolishly wise, they'll be the life and soul of the party, the joker, the charmer and the clown, trying to distract the family from its conflict and pain. Many of the world's comic geniuses are playing this role to perfection, but by trying so hard to make everyone happy they can't feel how cherished and loved they really are.

Do any of these sound familiar? Or can you think of other roles members of your family take on? Unless we challenge these outdated roles which were built on our childhood mistakes we will remain trapped in an unnecessary time warp. Remember, when we take on a role, any role, we are not being authentic. We're keeping people at a distance, rather like an actor in a television show who gets mistaken for his on-screen self. And don't forget that family roles fluctuate: you may be a hero one day and a martyr the next.

In order to create happiness for our families, we must first acknowledge the roles we have played and continue to play within the family and our adult life.

- Take a little time and look at the roles you played as a child.
- Which were your favourite ones?

Greta, an outgoing creative artist, finds it easy to run the home efficiently, manage her business successfully and maintain a good relationship with her husband Peter. In her quiet moments she even has time to plan how she would run the country. However, the moment she is with her family of origin something seems to change. She handles situations differently, her style of communication changes. She struggles not to slip back into a 'lost child' role and all that that entails. Her Ego Dramatist shouts, 'Remember what they did!' (reliving childhood fights) and, 'Don't smile, act sad!' (which was her old manipulative behaviour to get noticed).

Greta says it drives her mad to think she is an intelligent, capable 34-year-old woman, but in her mind she still feels like a seven-year-old with plaits and ribbons, hoping her older siblings will make it all better. It is as if her 15 years of adulthood never happened.

Anthony was the first child in a family of seven. He spent his formative years playing the hero role, helping his father in his business and running all the errands for his mother. He also helped to keep the other kids happy and quiet so as not to upset his parents' volatile relationship. He excelled in sports and received a scholarship, going on to become a successful businessman. If there were any problems among his siblings he would help them out financially and emotionally. Until one day he lost his business and his marriage fell to bits. The golden boy started to go downhill fast with alcohol and depression. Anthony never told his family any of this – he kept up the illusion that all was well in his life. He felt he couldn't ask for help, the role of hero was so entrenched.

Nowadays, Anthony has a good balanced relationship with his brothers and sisters – he learnt to let go of his role as helper and star. In fact his family was extremely willing and able to help him. Sometimes when the need to be needed is so great we lose ourselves.

Remember the High-Heeled Healer's dream of choosing our parents and siblings in heaven? This idea that we chose our family is sometimes a bitter pill to swallow. But if you accept that we chose to come to earth to learn a lesson as well as help others, our choice of parents and siblings makes sense. When you are unhappy with the result, remember it is all for a purpose – to complete your education and give your healing gifts. We hide them well when we feel threatened or misunderstood and mistakenly believe that life is meant to be a struggle.

As we get older, the roles we play in the family get in the way of the simple pleasures of life. We all start to fight for the special position, compete to be the best or the worst or the cleverest or the funniest or the loneliest, or even the most ill. The Ego Dramatist tells us there isn't enough love to go around, so best fight for your little bit of happiness. It says that to be happy you have to get appreciation and acknowledgement from the outside world. But this acts like a drug – you need higher and higher doses to feel 'happy'. The family, the place of nurturing, becomes a battle-ground for many little Egos.

- Think about your family. What role was your mum playing? Your dad? Grandma? Granddad?
- What family role is your partner playing?
- What gift could you give the martyr?
- What could you give the lost child?
- What could you give the hero?
- What could you give the entertainer?

- What could you give the trophy child?
- What could you give the scapegoat?

a meditation to heal your family

To follow on from the last exercise, here is a healing meditation that is a pleasure to do.

- First find a quiet spot. Sit down and close your eyes. Take a deep breath.
- Now release and relax your body ...
- Take another deep breath and relax your mind ...
- Imagine for a moment being in a place of great safety and love, a place where you can sit for a while and rest. Where would it be?
- Now imagine yourself in your personal sanctuary, a place designed by you, for you, a place to heal ...
- Now imagine being in a totally happy state, one where you are completely content ...
- Into this space invite a member of your family who has played a role that you perceived to be hurtful and wrong. (Alternatively, invite a member of your family for whom you believe the role you have been playing has been hurtful.)
- Who would that person be?
- Would you be willing to see them as innocent?
- Would you drop your defences and let them see you for who you are – drop the masks and roles?
- What do you see behind the façade? Walk towards them.
- What is it you need from them? Let them give you the gifts from their Backpack that have been hidden for so long ...
- Open your Backpack and your heart.
- What gifts do you have for them? What do you need to say to them?
- What would you like to hear them say to you? (It doesn't matter if they are back in heaven, the healing still happens.)
- Now relax and know that healing has happened and the world is now a kinder place and you have become happier and more authentic.

☆ don't worry, be happy

The bottom line is that the Ego leads us to believe that happiness depends on things outside ourselves. We think we have to wait until certain things are in place before we can be happy, but in fact happiness comes from within.

Simply by being happy you change the world. Smile at someone and see what I mean. Today, for no good reason, just choose to be happy. Spread happiness to two people who will then pass it on to two more. Tomorrow spread happiness to three people, who in turn will spread it to three more people. See how the world around you can change.

Being happy connects you to your inner wisdom and common sense. You have them, so why not use them? Being happy is also the greatest way to help others. When you have no happiness, you can't give happiness. When you have no love for yourself, you have no love to give others.

* Happiness is a form of love and can heal the worst pain.
* Happiness is infectious.
* Happiness is the best gift you can give the world.

☆ healerette's unhappy hour!

Your Ego Dramatist has probably found this chapter very difficult to deal with as all your unwanted feelings are surfacing. This is a good sign, as in order to clear the hidden sadness we must first confront it. Now I am suggesting that in place of the usual Healerette's Happy Hour we have an unhappy hour instead.

You may be well asking, 'Why is she trying to bring me down? This chapter is supposed to be about happiness!' Yep, it sure is, yet acknowledging your *negative* feelings is also part of the path to purpose, passion and adventure. You have probably never been given permission to feel down – normally we are given a pep talk and a dose of Prozac, then are expected to get up and get on with life – but there will be golden nuggets hidden in your gloom.

In the wonderful children's book *Winnie the Pooh* by A. A. Milne, there is a sad little donkey character called Eeyore. Eeyore never lets the optimism of Pooh the bear or Tigger the tiger sway him. He remains a killjoy. His predictable misery has earned him many fans. Now it is time to get in touch with your inner Eeyore! Today, give yourself permission to be Eeyore, to be the absolute worst whatever-it-is-you-want-to-be, to let loose the power that you have spent resisting Eeyoreitis. Indulge in misery. Ironically, it will probably bring you release, laughter and freedom. When you give yourself permission to break the rules, such a sweet honesty surfaces.

Are you trying to be a constantly upbeat, optimistic person? One reliable path to your goal is to dramatically become the opposite. Ignore all the blissful affirmations and joyful self-talk, just for a short time. You will find gold in the opposite. That may be why Eeyore has so many fans. Have some Eeyore moments. Don't be mildly glum and gloomy – give it your all. Be a theatrical, spectacular Drama Queen. Be the exact and true opposite of the lighthearted person you want to be.

If you have heard Eeyore's voice in a movie or video, you know how the donkey talks. Talk like Eeyore, too. Being Eeyore is fun. It is hard not to laugh when you are Eeyore-ing. Please give it a try. You'll get some giggles and a sharper focus on the kind of positive person you want to be. Playing the opposite somehow gives you that focus.

You know how it goes: 'I have to go and make a cup of tea now. I hope the milk's not gone off. I bet my partner's used the last tea bag. Yesterday I went shopping and the shopkeeper put the "Closed" sign up just when I wanted to buy some fresh milk and tea bags. Then I'll go for a walk, mind you the weather man said specifically there would be storms just where I live. Maybe I'll just go and get a newspaper, although why bother? It will be full of awful news. At least I will have my cup of tea.

I wonder where I can get one of those testers to make sure my water doesn't have lead in it…' Soon you'll start to have a great time. Your inner Eeyore will probably make you howl with laughter.

Go forth and have several Eeyore moments. Enjoy your moaning hour!

☆ healerette's happy hour

Now for some more positive but equally fun suggestions:

* ★ Re-read your favourite childhood book.
* ★ Hire a video of your favourite childhood movie and watch it with a bag of popcorn.
* ★ Sing at the top of your voice to your favourite old tape while you drive the car or while you're doing the housework.
* ★ Collect together some old family photos and make a collage – decide what roles you and your family were playing when the photo was taken. Look at the clothes you were all wearing – this alone is bound to raise a smile!

Chapter Four

peace

Obsessed by a fairy tale, we spend our lives searching for a magic door and lost kingdom of peace.
EUGENE O'NEILL

☆ checking out of heartbreak hotel

There once was a little girl who wanted more than anything to live happily ever after. All the fairy tales she'd read spoke of true love, romance and chivalry. In the books it seemed as though there were thousands of knights in shining armour ready and available to whisk damsels off their feet and take them to fairy castles in far-off lands where they would reign as queens and everyone in the land would love and admire them for their beauty, together with their ability to be calm and understanding. They would never grow old and their princes' eyes would never wander in the direction of the serving wenches. Queens never felt hurt, lonely or misunderstood; all their needs were met immediately without question. Parents-in-law loved the very ground they walked on and never had a cross word about the way they brought up the young princes and princesses. There were no money problems or fears or impending job losses.

As the ideal couple had never had any previous relationships, there was no jealousy or envy about past partners or feelings of abandonment or rejection, because they had both come from perfect parents – parents who had never had a cross word and loved and adored each other completely. In fact, they all got on so well they decided to share the same castle. In this far-off land there were no taxes, no politicians, no crime, no pollution, it never rained during the day and they all lived happily ever after.

I have many women and men in my workshops who have kissed frogs and froggettes galore looking for the ideal prince or princess, the one that will live up to the fairytale image. The belief is that if they are so-o-o good and so-o-o wonderful, if they never complain or argue and pretend that everything is OK, the prince or princess won't be able to live without them and everything will turn out fine. We now know that this isn't true. In this chapter we will delve into the secret myths behind romantic attraction and relationships and find the magic door of understanding and the lost kingdom of peace.

Here's another little fairy tale. A princess is put under a spell by a wicked fairy. The spell is that she will sleep for 100 years and so will all her servants and friends. The spell can only be broken by a true prince. Duly the prince arrives and kisses her; she wakes up to see this character in green tights and a codpiece. (She thinks, 'Oh, I can soon make him over.') What the story doesn't tell you is that the princess is often nearly 40 before she wakes up.

In my workshops I see many princes and princesses who want to wake up from the spell cast by the impossible goal of a fairytale romance. This chapter is your wake-up call – why sleep any longer?

For many of us the spell of romantic love has created a cycle in which we stumble and fall whenever we encounter a hurdle in a relationship. For some, the answer is to give up on having relationships altogether; for others it is to have a series of mini-marriages whereby they keep 'falling in love' too soon, hoping this time it will somehow work out right. Alternatively, we may just batten down the hatches and live through the façade of a happy dream, dreading the day when we have to admit to the outside world or to our families that all is not perfect.

Understanding the path of relationships and its pitfalls will help to rekindle the magic in a long-term relationship, allowing romance to return. In this chapter we will look at two key areas: the unsolved mystery of romantic attraction and how to declutter our relationship style and so attract a true partner.

☆ the unsolved mystery of romantic attraction

There are millions of theories as to why we choose a certain person to be romantically attracted to; here we will look at four of the more supported theories.

First, there is the 'biological' argument that states that men are subconsciously attracted to women they believe are capable of producing babies to carry on the species. In this scenario women are subconsciously attracted to men they think are able to provide for their babies.

A second theory is the socio-psychological 'exchange' theory in which we select partners who are more or less our equals, with similar backgrounds, schooling, financial and social standing.

A third idea is the 'personality' theory in which we choose a partner who enhances our self-esteem. There is often some truth in this – I know I have felt both very proud and on occasions extremely embarrassed because of the way I believed others perceived my guy. Then again, I think of the times he must have felt proud of and, at times embarrassed by, my outrageous behaviour. Oops!

The fourth, and often controversial, theory is the idea that we search for partners who resemble our parents or guardians. 'What?' I hear you cry. 'Do you mean to say that I am looking for a 60-year-old with no teeth, no hair and bad eyesight? Surely not!' But according to Harville Hendrix's 'Imago' theory, our choice of partner is not based on biological or socio-psychological logic, as the first three theories suggest. Hendrix argues that on a conscious level we look for people with only positive traits – people who are, among other things, kind, loving, good-looking, intelligent and creative. But no matter what our *conscious* intentions may be, most people are attracted to partners who have their parents' or guardians' positive *and* negative traits. Typically, the negative traits are more influential. Hendrix argues that when we fall in love it is always with someone who is similar to the parent with whom we had the most difficulty and who will frustrate us in a similar way to that parent.

When I talked about this in one of my seminars, a lady called Sally said to me, 'Is there no peace for the wicked? I have just sorted out my childhood racket with my siblings, only to find now I'm supposed to be looking for my dad? To clear my racket with him?' 'Yep!'

I must admit when I first worked with this theory I was pretty sceptical too. My first thought was 'Oh my God! Why would I want to do such a thing?' Yet, as I progressed along my path of discovery it all started to make sense. I began to think about past partners and how some of them ended up acting just like my dad, whereas with the others I was the one acting like him, poor lads. Armed with his new information, I went back to the drawing-board.

Hendrix's theory makes a lot of sense when you remember we choose our parents to learn lessons from and to share our gifts with. Unfortunately, as I described in the dream, on returning to earth we forget it all and hide those gifts in our Spiritual Backpacks. Our choice of partners gives us a second chance to heal with mum and dad and learn the lessons of relationship on a spiritual level. Although this looks like a formula for failure, in fact it contains the seeds of success in relationships.

☆ start by loving yourself

From the very moment we are born we are complex, dependent creatures with a never-ending cycle of needs. Even if we were lucky enough to have been raised in a loving, nurturing family, not all of our needs will have been met. No parent, no matter how dedicated, is able to respond quickly enough to attend to all of them. So we subconsciously look to our partners to provide the love or security we feel we did not receive as a child. But this is impossible. Our needs will never be met by another in quite the way we crave. We have to learn to take responsibility for ourselves. This is the absolutely key point from which to start building relationships. And it all starts with self-love.

Self-love doesn't mean we become selfish, it means that we appreciate our finer qualities. When I first heard this I thought, 'What finer qualities?' It is so much easier for us to list our negative qualities. But we have to nurture and value ourselves, for without this we can never have an intimate relationship. Instead we will manipulate and vampire all the brave souls that try to get close to us. But once we start to love ourselves, romance follows because we are ready to attract a loving partner.

We need to use the tools learned in Chapter Two, where we decluttered our homes and thoughts to allow room for progress. So it is with our relationships.

decluttering your relationships

In this section we will learn to declutter our relationships and lay the ghosts of Heartbreak Hotel to rest. We will give ourselves more excitement, understanding, authenticity and confidence, which will attract the same in return.

This section will provide a number of exercises in how to be truly available in order to attract an equal and loving partner. When I have used these exercises in workshops it is often hilarious to see people start to understand what they have actually been communicating to prospective partners.

Many of these ideas will be specifically aimed at relationships of an intimate nature. However, if you have any challenges with workmates, the exercises will still work just as well.

We will work on five areas:

* Laying the ghosts of the past to rest
* Exploring our relationship patterns
* Needs versus neediness
* Boundaries – saying 'yes' and meaning 'no'
* Do you believe a relationship will really make you happy?

laying the ghosts of the past to rest

The first secret of finding happiness in relationships is to make space for the 'ideal relationship'. Here we go again with our decluttering, only this time it is with our hearts.

Remember the racket we carry around with all our resentments, hurts and fears? All these heartbreaks are stored away as well and carried from one relationship to the next. As well as holding rackets, we are dragging huge invisible rubbish sacks of heartbreak along with us! Another point to ponder on is that the people we attract will have an equal amount of baggage. No wonder we get frightened of relationships. The sooner you can let go of your baggage, the less likely you are to create bad situations.

Use your intuition, your Miracle Mind, to provide the answers to the following questions.

■ Close your eyes and think about how many rubbish sacks you are dragging from relationship to relationship.
■ Can you see or hear any names being called out in relation to these sacks?
■ Whose name is it?

- What did they do?
- What didn't they do?
- Make a list of all the resentments you are still holding on to.
- Put the list into the imaginary sack.
- Imagine you had a special friend or angel who would take these old pains and sacks of hurt away.
- Would you be willing to hand the sacks over to this friend?
- Do it now and feel the peace.
- What lesson did you learn from the relationship you've just let go?
- What was that person's gift to you?
- Can you now receive it?
- And what gift did you withhold from them?
- Is it time to share your gift? Remember the universal laws – what you give you will receive.

To move on in our lives we have to be complete. By that I mean having no loose ends tied to our heart, otherwise if a similar scenario happens, our heartstrings will be pulled immediately. That's why letting go of the past is vitally important.

Being complete with your past has two key benefits. First, when certain circumstances cause you pain you become free to choose how to act rather than just react. Second, you no longer have an emotional reaction when remembering the past hurt. I can't stress too strongly how important it is to let go of old baggage if you want to have an intimate relationship. If you are holding on to Tom, Dick and Harry there isn't much space for Mr Wonderful, is there?

Here are four suggestions for dealing with any past hurt, rejection or guilt about relationships and moving on.

the unsent letter

Write as many letters as you want to the person, freely saying everything you want to say to feel complete. Do not send them. Instead, create a little ritual of burning them. When I do this exercise with any kind of hurt, I watch as the smoke rises in the air. Afterwards I feel so much freer. When I finally received my divorce papers, I put all the correspondence in a metal bucket and burnt every piece of paper. It took hours, but with every letter I felt my energy lift.

set up a peace pow wow

Talk to the person with whom you feel you still have unfinished business. (Only do this, though, if you know they will be able to listen to you.) Make sure you do not blame them or play the victim. *Don't* go for a quick slurp on a sympathy pitch about your sad life or, on the other hand, rave on about how great it's been since you split up. Talk about your feelings and remember to listen to what they have to say about the episode. It may be easier now there is some space between you. Never miss an opportunity to shut up and listen. Every episode in life is a potential lesson. If the chance is there, have as many conversations as you need to reach a completion.

pray

Ask your Miracle Mind to take this hurt and anger away. It is extremely powerful to ask every day: 'Please remove the resentment/judgement/ anger and blame I am feeling towards [name] and all our misunder-standings. Please give [name] peace and forgiveness.' As you send them peace and forgiveness you will receive peace and forgiveness back tenfold.

talk to the spirits!

Sometimes it is difficult to imagine the person standing still long enough to say hello, let alone have a conversation with them. In times like these, or if there has been violence, or if they have passed away, it's best to have a conversation with their spirit. You may think it may not be able to hear you, but it will.

As you do these exercises an unimaginable field of possibilities will unfold. You will free yourself and your partner from the past. You will be free to form new friendships with people based on your authentic self. You will be able to see the essence and beauty of others and so attract a more equal partner.

exploring our relationship patterns

Partnership patterns are formed in childhood. It is called 'unconscious patterning'. There are no rights or wrongs, it just happens that way. We are not going to pick on, or complain about, our parents here – they had their own roles, troubles and dreams that weren't fulfilled. They probably followed their own parents' style, which may not have worked for them either. Many couples in our parents' generation didn't have the time to take an inventory of who they were. We are lucky to be able to take the time to know our true selves.

There's a story about a young married couple who wanted to do everything right. They invited her parents over for dinner. The young man, John, was helping his wife, Janet, to prepare roast pork.

John said, 'I have wanted to ask you this for a long time. Why do you cut off the two ends of the pork?'

Janet replied, 'I have always seen my mother doing it. I'll ask her.'

Janet went into the lounge and asked: 'Mum, John wants to know why we cut off the two ends of the roast pork. I couldn't explain it. Why do you do it?'

Janet's mother answered, 'Well, darling, I don't really know either. Your grandmother always did it, so you'd better ask her.'

Later Janet rang her grandmother. 'Hello, Gran. Can you tell me why you cut off the two ends of the roast pork for best results? Mother could not explain it.'

Gran replied: 'My child, I always did it that way because the pork could not fit into my cooking pot.'

Just like Janet and her mother before her we do many things automatically without knowing their origin. What are you doing in your life that may be along the same lines as cutting the ends off roast pork? I think it would be worth checking. Maybe you are constantly attracting unsuccessful relationships because of some family pattern.

As I keep saying throughout the book, accountability is paramount. Accountability protects your heart and soul. Look at your patterns honestly. If past partnerships haven't worked out, take responsibility for your part in their failure. Don't allow the victim role to raise its wimpy little head – you will give all your power away.

Take a little step back in time to Heartbreak Hotel. Whatever is stored there in your subconscious mind is buried alive. We relive the past every time we get hurt because the feelings and thoughts aren't dead, they are just locked away. Roaming around Heartbreak Hotel, we're haunted by these hidden events, feelings and reactions, but unaware of the impact they have on our conscious thoughts and patterns.

Decluttering your Heartbreak Hotel takes three stages, so get your heart broom ready to make a clean sweep.

1. Take an Inventory

- In your journal list the names of three significant others. (Significant relationships are those you had, or still have, strong feelings about.) The relationships may have been years ago, it doesn't matter. What you are looking for is the patterns. Starting with the most recent, write down your answers to these questions: What didn't work? What hurtful things did your partner do in the relationship?
- Ask the same questions with partner two.
- And again with partner three.

Jinny, a client, realized after doing this exercise that her last three guys had behaved in similar ways, which always triggered the same behaviour from her. She felt that they worked all the time and were emotionally unavailable. Her pattern was to finish with them and within a few months move on to another guy with exactly the same traits. All she had really done was to change heads.

Jinny acknowledged that this was wake-up time. She had to get these patterns cleared once and for all, otherwise, she had decided, the only answer was to give up on men and go off to become a nun. Well, I had to get to work quickly – Jinny wasn't really nun material. She needed to change her relationship habits rather than take on the habit of a nun.

Jinny realized that her issue was not so much that her boyfriends were workaholics but that she had *chosen* them for this quality and then placed on them demands that they could never meet. I am glad to report that after taking this honest inventory of her past she started to attract much more available partners.

2. Get Out the Childhood Snapshots

Where do these relationship patterns come from? In order to answer this question we must look deeper into our childhood memories. These provide us with our 'snapshots' from the past.

In the case of Jinny, I asked her some questions about her family:

* 'What unkind things did your father do to your mother?'
* *'He was emotionally unavailable.'*
* 'What upsetting things did your mum do to your dad?'
* *'She worked all the time and ignored him.'*
* 'What insensitive things did your dad do to you?'
* *'He never showed me any affection.'*
* 'What hurtful things did your mum do to you?'
* *'She was always busy. I never felt valued or loved.'*

The similarities between the hurtful behaviour of Jinny's partners and her parents' style of relationship are all too obvious.

Take a look at your own parents' style. Ask yourself the questions I asked Jinny and see what family behaviour is sabotaging your relationships. These family styles come in many forms and are closely linked to the roles we explored in the previous chapter. For example if you played deputy mum or dad and had to take care of the family, you may find yourself always taking care of your partner; if you grew up as the lost child in a family of anger or violence, you may avoid any conflict or constantly bicker and complain; and so on.

   As you identify the roles you used to protect yourself in the past, can you see how that pattern of behaviour interferes with intimacy in any relationship?

3. Get Out the Mirror

If we choose to, we can see our relationships as a way of understanding ourselves. Pick up the mirror, not a microscope, when you start to complain about your partner. Have you ever noticed that the words 'parent' and 'partner' have the same letters? Partner has an extra 'r' for responsibility – our ability to respond as an adult, not as a child.

   As we've just seen, when we are children, the adults around us act as role models and it is logical for us to believe that theirs is the only way to behave in a relationship. We become their mini-mes and trophy children. Alternatively, we see their relationship as disaster areas and swear we will never ever be like them. Either way, we all end up catching ourselves saying or doing the very thing that we found most annoying as a child. How many times have you said something to your partner or your child and thought 'I sound just like my mum'?

   It is not always that our actions are the same as our parents' – in some cases they are the opposite – but the outcome may be equally damaging. (There is no blame here – remember from the High-Heeled Healer's dream that we chose our parents to learn lessons from. Some of us took on a monumental task and yet are succeeding. Well done!)

Here are a few more questions to ask yourself. Take these exercises light-heartedly as they are designed to free old limiting behaviour. Think of the fun you'll have when you've finally checked out of Heartbreak Hotel.

- Are you repeating your parents' relationship in your relationships?
- Do your partners ever point out to you that you are just like one of your parents? Or vice versa, do you say the same to them?
- Did you ever promise yourself you would never behave like your parents? And do you still behave like them?
- When your partner does anything remotely resembling hurtful behaviour from the past, do you sulk for days, months or even years?
- Earlier in the chapter, I introduced four letting-go exercises: the unsent letter, the peace pow wow, the prayer, spirit talk. Which one would you choose to help you move on?

Once you understand the origin of your relationship pattern you can take action to change it. Remember, your parents had shattered dreams too. They were looking for their needs to be met by another person. Can you imagine for a minute how they thought their lives would be? What was the dream your mum had as a young girl? What was it your dad wanted for his young wife and child?

Disappointment can be inherited. As children, when we see our parents disappointed, sad or unhappy, we often feel we are responsible. We then take on their pain, which leads to disenchantment. Often we don't know why we feel sad, which is not really surprising when you realize that the sadness is not really ours. Forgiveness means letting go of pain. Forgiveness finishes unfinished business by tying up loose ends and allowing for new beginnings. Forgiveness releases you and the person you are judging. As you forgive you create space in your heart, allowing room for a more equal partner to wing their way to you.

Jinny let go of her old snapshots and checked out of Heartbreak Hotel. She understood that she came to this planet to give the gifts of love and value to her parents, and as she did this she received a sense of being valued and loved in return. Jinny now knows that one person alone cannot be expected to fulfil all her needs. That is not to say she does not have needs – we all do. What we must do now is find out what our true needs are and how they can be met with integrity.

needs versus neediness

All of us have needs and that's OK! When we are in a relationship we sometimes think or feel that the significant other will fulfil all our needs, and I can tell you that our new partner is thinking exactly the same about us. So from a loving romantic start, we end up as two needy people denying that we have needs. And we wonder why our relationships are such a mess.

There is *not one person* on the planet who can fulfil all your needs all of the time. It is impossible. If a person ever does fulfil all your needs, it can only be for a short time because they have to take on such a sacrificial role to do this that the relationship is doomed from day one.

Remember the racket that we use to push people away when a relationship starts to become serious and all our fears about commitment and intimacy come up? Remember also that our partner will have their own racket created by their own particular needs, misunderstandings and ghosts? For a relationship to blossom and grow we must be honest with ourselves and our partner as to what our needs are.

Sometimes it is hard to be specific. Especially if when we were growing up we were told that our needs didn't count or we were selfish if we voiced them: 'I want never gets.' As a result we never learnt to put words to our needs. We may only have a vague idea of what will make us feel better, happy or more fulfilled. But being ambiguous about our needs doesn't help us to attract an equal partner. It means we could be waiting years for a partner who miraculously has the psychic ability to read our mind.

The following exercise will help you to discover and express your needs.

Take some time now to really think about what would make you happy. What would you like in your life? Many people find this exercise difficult at first because they are not used to listening to their needs or wants. They think it's selfish – but this exercise isn't about being selfish, it's about valuing yourself. The questions are:

- What would make me feel good today?
- What do I want?
- What do I need?
- From whom? (Myself? Someone else?)
- In what way? (To hear something, to be held, to be acknowledged? To give love? To receive love? What form would it take?)
- How will I know my want or need has been met?

Every morning list your answers on an index card. Put your list in your purse or pocket – a somewhere that is easily accessible – and take it with you everywhere. Practise checking in with yourself throughout the day about how you feel and what would make you feel better.

Defining your needs, putting them into words, may be a new experience for you. Have patience and keep practising. Doing this exercise regularly could change your whole perception of life. You will develop a more defined sense of yourself – and new respect for both yourself and your needs.

Leonora rang me to say that she'd had enough of her live-in lover. He never took her anywhere, he had lived with her for four years and they hardly communicated any more, He didn't believe in a spiritual path and she did. He said that he wanted children and she couldn't have any. She was always expecting him to leave. And to top the lot he was now using the spare bedroom as an office to run his business. She said she was swinging between being a dictator and being a doormat and she wanted to change.

I asked her what needs she thought he could fulfil when she met him. She told me that they had never discussed each other's needs, because she hadn't known how to ask for what she wanted. She had kept her fingers crossed, hoping that one day he would understand what she wanted through her silences and sighs. We discussed how in our minds we write a script of how the relationship should be and never tell the partner. All the rules we have are in code and small print, which the partner never has sight of. Leonora had presumed her guy was a mystic or a clairvoyant when in fact he was a glazier. I asked her to list 16 needs she had thought the mystic glazier could fulfil when they first met. This was her list:

Loyalty, touch, communication, sex, acknowledgement, love, companionship. A spiritual partner. Adventure. Equal share of the bills. Help around the house. Nurturing. Cheap double-glazed windows. To talk about feelings, dreams and careers. Fidelity. To be a playmate. Lots of hugs …

Leonora had so many needs that her boyfriend could never possibly have met them. He could only meet a few. The next thing I asked her to do was to tick five needs he could easily meet. She was to try and get the rest of her needs met by herself, her friends and those close to her.

In defining your needs, you must also learn to identify the difference between your requirements, your functional needs and your emotional needs:

* ⋆ *Requirements* are core basic needs that are often relationship-breakers if unmet, such as fidelity, having children, sharing step-children, spirituality.
* ⋆ *Functional needs* are the things you need to happen for your life and relationship to function easily, such as earning enough money to pay the bills, sharing the everyday jobs around the home, discussing your tolerations.

★   *Emotional needs* are what you need to feel loved, such as hugs, touch
and acknowledgement. You may need to hear terms of endearment
such as 'I love you' or to be shown you are loved by receiving cards
or flowers.

▪   List ten needs you want met in a relationship.
▪   Now list three needs that are must-haves in a long-term relationship.
▪   Of the remaining seven needs on the list, which of these can be met by you
    or others close to you?

Our ability to identify our needs and get them met determines our level
of happiness and success. Until your needs are met you really can't make
the most of all your gifts.

Neediness tends to be like a sieve that will be empty regardless of how
much you put into it. Below are the differences between needs and
neediness.

needs

★   are normal, valid, important and not a sign of weakness.
★   are present in everyone, including healthy, successful people.
★   are necessary to survive and thrive.
★   are best met by taking responsibility and showing initiative – being
    accountable.
★   bring you contentment when met.

neediness

★   often comes from unmourned loss.
★   means we depend on another to make us happy.
★   results in us playing victim and sacrificer roles.
★   results in manipulation and emotional blackmail.
★   is like trying to fill a black hole in space – it's an impossible task.

Try these suggestions whenever you feel your needs are becoming neediness:

- Recognize what makes you needy. For example, Leonora recognized that she felt needy when she didn't communicate with her partner.
- Have a set plan of what to do when you start to feel needy. Leonora learnt that her glazier wasn't psychic and started to communicate verbally about her needs.
- If you are in a place of neediness and you don't know what to do, call on your Miracle Mind and ask the question, 'Who needs *my* help?' Intuitively a name will come to you. Phone the person or write a note or maybe just send love. When you are on your knees in pain there is always somebody in need of your help.

We need to take responsibility for our needs and not rely on a partner to meet them. We can be loved by someone who may not fulfil all our needs.

The reality is that relationships may fail altogether if we haven't discussed what our needs are or refuse to meet any of our partners' needs. Remember not to expect your partner to know what's going on inside your mind. Tell them what you want and don't forget to ask what they want from you. Be willing to negotiate so both of you are satisfied; this is a step towards intimacy and will take you to a new level of partnership.

boundaries – saying 'yes' and meaning 'no'

Boundaries are invisible energy lines that protect us. They are there to keep hazards and hurts at bay. We need to be able to create healthy boundaries so as not to feel totally swamped by other people's needs. By having boundaries we are honouring ourselves and letting others know how to behave around us. When we have strong boundaries and make them known to a potential partner they have some idea of what they can and cannot do. This in turn makes us more discerning and deserving of respect from others.

When you feel your boundaries are threatened, say to yourself, 'Deflector shields up,' just as they say in *Star Trek* when they go into uncharted territories or feel under attack. We can show our boundaries in our vocabulary too. 'Yes' and 'no' are the two most powerful words we have. We create our lives by these two words. When we say 'yes' to something we go in one direction and when we say 'no' we head in another.

Do you have a hard time saying 'no'? Many of us do. So what do we do instead? We say 'yes'! How many times have you said 'yes' and then beat yourself up for being weak, or felt as guilty as sin because you didn't want to do the task you volunteered for? Then you have to spend precious time making silly excuses. And if you do ever finish the task it's usually less than your best attempt. Have you ever said 'yes' to your partner and then gone straight into sacrificer mode because you made their needs more important than your own? If we don't keep our boundaries clear to ourselves, how can anybody else know where these invisible lines are?

When we let people step over our boundary lines we feel drained immediately. So why do we do it? For most of us saying 'no', *non* or *nein* is contrary to what we have been taught. We have been taught that it's not polite to say 'no', even if saying 'yes' is damaging to us.

We can learn to say 'no' by trusting our intuition. When I am asked to commit to something I always tell the person I will get back to them shortly. It gives me time to ask myself if it is my truth: 'Do I feel as though this is a sacrifice? Will I only be doing this to look good? Am I giving to get?' Then I wait to see what emotions come up. Once I started saying 'no' more often, people started to respect my boundaries and treat me differently.

Practise saying 'no'. Start with little things until you get comfortable. If you've been playing any kind of role which involves trying to please everybody, you may feel guilty. But it's only your Ego Dramatist trying to vamp your energy. 'No' can be a complete sentence. You don't have to make up an excuse to support it. Say 'no' out loud now. The more you practise it, the less guilt you'll feel. The energy thieves in your life may get a shock at first, but just keep stepping into your power, and remember 'Deflector shields up!'

A really good way to learn to do this is to watch a friend who has strong boundaries. Watch their style and mannerisms. Model them, note every detail. How do they speak? How do they stand? What is the difference between your body language and theirs? How do people treat them?

Always remember the dynamic duo of accountability and choice. Take responsibility for your life. Even the best partners will do something that will not be OK with you. Let them know if it's affecting you negatively. Most partners would love some guidelines. It's a minefield trying to find out if certain behaviour is OK. Give them guidelines about time, sex, money, family, food, health. I am sure you would appreciate some feedback yourself too. Are you aware of crossing other people's boundaries? The more aware you are of others' boundaries, the stronger your own boundaries become. Learn to value yourself and your space.

Setting boundaries isn't a control issue; it's a self-love issue.
ANON

five benefits of setting boundaries

* Boundaries enhance your ability to select the right partner. The wrong partners will cross your boundaries early on in the relationship. If you are aware of your boundaries it will save you months of procrastinating about their behaviour.
* When you're being true to yourself and your own boundaries, you naturally feel more generous to others.
* You are giving yourself the freedom to do the things that are important to you – to live your own life at last.
* You trust yourself more and consequently others trust you more.
* You feel empowered. It's always empowering when you are being true to yourself.

To know and honour your boundaries increases your self-esteem while earning the respect of others. There are probably many times and ways we have let people trample over our boundaries in a relationship, even though Quasimodo from *The Hunchback of Notre Dame* is ringing every alarm bell in our head. Many failed relationships are the result of singles seeking to meet their immediate physical and emotional needs and not learning the skills of creating boundaries. Remember that *you* are the most important person in your life. Ideally, you are gently educating people about who you are and what you want. That gives you confidence – and there is nothing sexier than a confident person.

do you really believe a relationship will make you happy?

The reason many of us are unable to say 'no' is because we have a hidden belief that saying 'no' will make us unlovable. Yes, those old hidden beliefs rear their ugly heads once again! Let's see how they work in terms of our relationships.

During a workshop in Manchester in which we were exploring the theory that happiness is the best revenge, Petra, a well-built girl from Wigan, sat glaring at me with her arms crossed and her legs crossed, looking as though she'd just swallowed a wasp. Not a happy bunny at all. This was definitely negative body language and it didn't take a rocket scientist to work it out. In this hostile atmosphere I broached the subject of hidden beliefs about relationships and in particular about the opposite sex.

I asked the participants to write down the first thing that came to mind on the five subjects below.

If you want to try this exercise, write the answers down in your journal.

▩ Men are...

- Men are ...
- Men are ...
- Men are ...
- Men really are ...

- Women are ...
- Women are ...
- Women are ...
- Women are ...
- Women really are ...

Then do the same exercise with 'relationships', 'sex' and 'love'.

This is how Petra answered:

- '*Men* are pigs, a***holes, liars. Men really are losers.'
- '*Women* are strong, loyal, bitches, trustworthy. Women really are loving.'
- '*Relationships* are hard work, up and down, hurtful, don't last. Relationships really are important.'
- '*Sex* is quick, Friday night, sticky, great with the right person. Sex really is a way of showing love.'
- '*Love* is warm, belonging, important, hard to hold on to. Love really is what living is all about.'

Believe it or not, this is pretty typical of the answers around the world. The second part of the exercise is to change the words 'men', 'women', 'relationships' and 'sex' to 'I am...' I know I am cheating a little here, but what we see in others is what we believe about ourselves on a very hidden and deep level.

I asked Petra if she was in a relationship. She said that she wasn't, but she had been looking and there were no decent or available men around. I went on to explain to the group that when a man or a woman walks into the room and we have these negative thoughts about their gender, we send out little spiky energy arrows that they can somehow sense as an attack. These potential mates are very wary of the black widow spider in the corner of the club, restaurant or wine bar. They have heard horror stories from their friends about how they were invited to lunch by this sexy spider woman only to find out that they *were* the lunch and would be devoured at a later date.

So even though Petra was out looking for a partner, energetically she was saying: 'Pigs, a***holes, liars, losers!' And attached to every word was a spiky arrow heading straight towards any available men in the vicinity.

Luckily Petra told me she was willing to try something new, so we did an exercise called 'The Relationship Bucket'. I asked her to name three past lovers. She mentioned the well-known trio of Tom, Dick and Harry. I then asked her to intuit or just make up three numbers between 1 and 100. She replied: 'Tom 67%, Dick 79% and Harry 96%.'

Before you read any further, try this exercise. Just like Petra, jot down the name of three past lovers. Give each of them a number between 1 and 100.

- Lover number one ... %
- Lover number two ... %
- Lover number three ....%

Now add them up. Petra's total was 245%. What was yours? Another sneaky question? Perhaps! But it shows you energetically how much you are holding on to past lovers. If your total was 50%, it means you are only 50% available; if your total was 85%, you are only 15% available. If your total was anything over 100%, there is very little room for a new relationship.

Look at Petra's total: 245%, a high number by any standard. She was definitely ready to let Tom, Dick and Harry go. Tom (67%) was her first love and she had treated him really badly. I asked her if she could forgive herself there and then and imagine letting him go. She said yes, it was time to move on and stop beating herself up about it.

We did the same exercise with Dick on 79% and Harry on 96%. After the exercise Petra looked so much softer. Letting go is one of our most valuable healing gifts. There is no problem that does not involve some form of holding on or attachment. Try the same exercise yourself and see what a difference it can make to how you feel.

As the day progressed Petra completed all the exercises in this chapter. At the end of the day she looked like a different woman. Gone were the wasp lips and the negative body language. She even had a new mantra: 'Men are magic! Men are magic! Men are magic!'

☆ so what do you want in a relationship?

This is the exciting part. Now you have a better idea of who you are, you will also have a better picture or feeling of what you want in a partner and a relationship. Do you still dream of being saved by a knight in a suit of rusty armour that needs oiling and polishing regularly? And don't forget the trusty steed – it needs mucking out daily. If you live in a fairy tale, the relationship will never last the test of time.

Here are a few questions to ponder in your journal before we take the next step towards an intimate loving relationship:

- What three things make you thrive in a relationship?
- Are you setting your standards too low?
- What behaviour will you definitely never tolerate again?
- What behaviour of yours has sabotaged relationships in the past?
- Will you be more aware when the red flag pops up, letting you know you are reacting to the past and not the present?

After completing all these exercises you will be well on your way to meeting the right mate. Once you meet that one and only you will step onto the path of relationship. In the next chapter I will help you to avoid the rocky patches and most common pitfalls.

☆ this way out of heartbreak hotel

Congratulations on working your way through this chapter and checking out of Heartbreak Hotel. Hopefully you have gained an insight into yourself, released a number of the stressed-out strings in your racket, dumped some sacks of rubbish and used some of those precious gifts that you have been hiding in your Backpack.

Having successfully completed the exercises in this chapter you will feel more at peace as well as empowered to take the next step onto the magical path of relationships. It will amaze you how the path unfolds and how nature takes a hand with many twists and turns that keep us on our toes.

☆ healerette's happy hour

As this chapter was all about decluttering your relationships and understanding yourself more, your head and heart will have had quite a workout. So have fun with your senses this week. Each day choose consciously to explore a different sense for ten minutes two or three times during the day. For example:

* On Monday, sit with your eyes closed and focus only on the sounds around you – those close up, those a short distance away, those in the distance.
* On Tuesday have an exotic snack in a shopping centre where you can taste many different types of food or try a food you have never tasted before.
* On Wednesday collect a box of new scents and smells. You can get many free samples from the perfume counters in town

* On Thursday assemble a collection of varied textures: wool, silk, cotton, linen, wood, metal. Close your eyes and simply feel the textures and enjoy the touch.
* On Friday take a walk around a natural area of beauty close to where you live or work. Simply enjoy seeing and perceiving.
* At the weekend flick through some old magazines, cutting out pictures representing peace and tranquillity – a beach at dawn, a forest in spring, a snow-laden Christmas scene, clouds, anything that makes you feel relaxed. Make them into an attractive collage and put them in your journal. Reflect on these images and allow yourself to feel at peace – you deserve it.

Chapter Five

love and romance

A man walks down the street and falls into a hole.
A man walks down the street, sees the hole and falls into it.
A man walks down the street, sees the hole and walks around it.
A man walks down a different street.
ANON

A desire for the right relationship is a natural part of life. It is the quest for 'the other half', the 'one and only', 'the beloved'. We dream of the possibilities and the passion of joining with a 'soul mate', somebody who will understand us and cherish our hearts.

A relationship is a living, growing, complex joint venture. Contrary to popular belief, good relationships don't just 'happen'. They require time, love and effort. Relationships progress through recognizable stages. All relationships experience crises and demand at least some flexibility from both partners. To have a good relationship we need commitment and a willingness to stay together through the rough and the smooth. With this in mind, let us look at the path of relationship.

Armed with the map and compass that is this chapter, you will find it far easier to steer clear of the many potholes and pitfalls that mark the path to a great and abiding love and friendship. I wish I had had this map when I was younger. All my life, all I ever wanted was to be loved. I never realized that I didn't know the first thing about love, or for that matter, relationships.

I remember going to the cinema with my first love, Johnny, to watch Zeffereli's *Romeo and Juliet*. The film was about relationships, passion, intrigue, deceit, misunderstandings, star-crossed lovers and a family feud. Sound familiar? It could have been any modern-day soap opera. Johnny and I never stayed to see the end of the film. We knew Romeo and Juliet would set up an intricate plot to be together, just like we had. What we didn't know was that it all goes terribly wrong and they both die for love. At 17 we believed we were in love. We were innocent, naïve and blinded by the dream. We thought we could 'make it'. I have since wondered whether if I had stayed to see the end of the film my daughter would have been conceived. And if not, how different would my life have been?

So, at the age of 17 I was married and pregnant. I thought I had all the answers. He loved me. I was true. We would have a little house and a couple of babies and life would be sweet – duh! The notion of the Romeo and Juliet-type love is a trap many of us fall into. A romantic tragedy in which we will stand together against the world... Unfortunately, my marriage lasted about as long as the film. As a single parent I had to learn quickly to be mum, dad and breadwinner. The loss and fear I felt were soon hidden by my new role, that of an 18-year-old independent single parent. I decided I had to do it all alone; I hid the feelings of abandonment and betrayal underneath my party-girl role and painted on a smile as though I didn't care. But underneath the painted smile was a broken dream. I closed down my heart and stopped believing in love. I made a decision to be in control and never to feel that vulnerable again. I thought by closing down I would not get hurt again. Wrong move. By closing down the bad feelings, we also close down the good ones. My emotions did not disappear, they just became part of my racket.

As a teenager, what did I know? There were no relationship classes; all I had was my limited view of the world. I never realized that my own wants and needs were valid. Boundaries? What boundaries? I didn't have any. I didn't know how to value my gifts or myself. I didn't know about my Spiritual Backpack. Relationship patterns? Patterns in those days would have meant knitting patterns. Terms like 'hidden beliefs' and 'roles' were not in my vocabulary. If at 15 or 16 years old I had had access to a map that explained the path of relationship, one which signposted the potholes and pitfalls, I would probably have chosen differently.

At that time, I had no idea what relationships were really about. I thought that when the romance ended it was over. *Next!* Yet through relationships we can learn not just to be happy but also to heal the hurt, loss, rejection and betrayal of the past through commitment, love, forgiveness and understanding.

Many people can only give enough of themselves to attract a mate and do not have a clue how to sustain a loving relationship. That's why it's so important to explore your own behaviour. When you are ready, you will attract a person who knows or is willing to learn how to build a relationship on a firm foundation.

Down the ages, the search for love and romance has inspired poems, songs, plays, musicals and films. We read the books, listen to the songs, watch the films, play the tapes and even go to the seminars. In my seminars, the questions are always the same: 'Is there a soul mate for me?' 'How do we keep the romance alive?' 'Will I get bored?' 'Will they get bored with me?' 'How do I know they are the right mate for me?' 'Will it last?' 'How do I cope with my jealousy?' 'How can I let go of my past pain?' In order to answer these questions we must go deeper into why we continually fall into certain traps – the traps that lead us back into the old insecurities.

After a monumental amount of research both inside and out I began to recognize some of the tricks, traps and temptations that trip us all up on the path to love. From Adam and Eve through Samson and Delilah to Cleopatra and Mark Antony lovers around the world and through the ages have made the same mistakes, dragging their relationships into their own personal Ego Dramas.

Some of the traps in this chapter you will recognize. Maybe you have used them on unsuspecting dates … or been on the receiving end of them. What is certain is that we repeatedly use certain recognizable forms of behaviour that emotionally entrap others. Tricks, traps and temptations will stop a relationship from blossoming. Below is a list of 12 commonly used traps. When you evaluate your own style you may be surprised at how many of these you use.

☆ the twelve traps

1. the fast love trap

This is when the couple constantly text message each other throughout the day with special lovey-dovey names like 'Pussykins' and 'Big Boy'. They want to be with each other every spare moment, drown each other in flowers, cards and compliments and indulge in completely inappropriate over-the-top displays of affection in public. They push the relationship forward quickly, demanding that it goes deeper. These are all signs that you're caught in the trap of fast love. Fast love makes you feel extremely good, but it's impossible to sustain. The high is incredible and it is possible to become addicted to it But the reality is that it takes years to really get to know someone. One of the gifts of being human is our complexity. It is impossible to know someone in a few dates or a week or from a text message. You cannot reveal your fragile heart until you feel safe.

How long does it take you to truly know someone? Be aware that your date will have a hidden agenda as well. Both of you should make a list of your needs in a short-term and a long-term relationship. Remind yourself of the needs versus neediness list in Chapter Four. Discuss your lists with each other. If your partner won't sit down long enough to complete the list, alarm bells should be ringing.

2. the marketing trap

Here, we believe we need to make ourselves more appealing to attract a partner and to 'sell' ourselves with attractive packaging and presentation. This approach always carries a high risk of disappointment and failure as partners discover that the promise of the 'exciting, sexy red convertible' conflicts with the reality of the 'clapped-out old Volvo estate'. The truth is that to attract a true partner you don't have to be young, slim and the height of fashion. The most attractive quality we have is self-esteem and the confidence that it carries.

If you regularly fall into the marketing trap I urge you to look at yourself and identify what makes you unique. What makes you the special individual that you are? Make a list of adjectives that describe you, such as 'funny', 'inspiring', 'smart', 'attractive' and so forth. Consider sharing your list with a close and trusted friend. Ask them to be honest and to add or take off any adjectives that over-enhance or undermine you. Are you being realistic or are you playing the chameleon and adapting to what you believe is required to market yourself? When you become authentic through self-awareness and self-acceptance, there is no doubt you will attract the kind of people you want to be with.

3. the soul-mate trap

Here, we immediately start looking for signs that fate has brought us together and are amazed at any little coincidence in the path of our lives. Some clients are convinced they have been together in a past life. 'We fell in love at first sight.' 'We committed to each other right away.' 'It is as if we have known each other all our lives.'

In the soul-mate trap you will look for someone with whom you can feel at home right away, someone who will understand you and give you what you need immediately. You feel a sense of recognition, connection and deep attraction. Interpreting a strong attraction to someone as a sign that this relationship is 'meant to be' is doomed to failure.

You will probably not know your 'soul mate' right away. You will not hear a fanfare of trumpets from celestial beings. You will only know them by a very gentle tug on your heart.

Sit and list how many 'soul mates' you have had in your life. Write the stories of what happened and what went wrong. This list alone should bring you back to earth with a bump.

4. the changing heads trap

Here, when a relationship ends you find a new person and get into a new relationship straight away. You hate being alone, you are hurting and you feel desperate about not having someone to share your life with. You feel being alone is a punishment or a torture. This trap isn't fair on the new unsuspecting substitute; you are unavailable to love them. Give yourself a grieving period. At the end of a relationship it is natural to need time to reflect and heal. You will come to realize that this is a gift, an opportunity to get to know yourself. It gives you strength and a chance to understand why the relationship failed and to come to terms with that. Then and only then are you ready for a new relationship.

Pasha, a divorced client, quickly started a new relationship after his ten-year marriage to Sandra ended. This strategy, he believed, would help him forget his wife. He was amazed at how easily he slipped into a new relationship. But his new liaison with Leticia lasted only a few months and although he admitted to having very strong feelings for her after they split up, he immediately jumped into yet another relationship with an unsuspecting substitute. In fact, the strong feelings Pasha had for Leticia were actually nothing to do with her. They were old emotions that he had been dragging around with him ever since his divorce, and even before that.

Emotions start to seep through everything we do until we address them. When we try to push away the grieving process all that happens is that it becomes a heavy weight in the heart. Pasha decided to take it a lot more slowly with substitute number two and have a meeting with Sandra, his ex-wife, to clear up the unanswered questions about why their marriage hadn't worked out.

There is a commonly held but mistaken belief that the only way to forget a former relationship and avoid facing feelings of grief is to enter a new one. But this strategy means we hold our needs, wants and desires trapped in our hearts, unfelt, unmet and lying in wait for the next partner. If we do not allow ourselves to feel the effects of a break-up we will just go and recreate the same mistakes all over again. If you want something different, a fulfilling relationship, you have to allow yourself to feel.

If constantly changing partners is one of your traps, try a period of celibacy. Ninety days ought to do the trick. This breather will help to clear some of the old emotional baggage.

This is one for your journal:

- How do you feel about your past relationships?
- Have you pushed your feelings away?
- Are you still secretly pining for someone?

5. the amnesia trap

The belief here is that if you develop an exclusive relationship with someone you are dating, a successful committed relationship will eventually happen. So you drop all your friends, forget about your dreams and needs, stop looking after yourself and forget you had a life before the relationship. The problem here is that forgetting takes a ton of energy to maintain. And we can only suppress our emotions, reactions and needs for so long. Eventually, our real self will start showing through and shocking the person we are with. This approach is what I call a WOMBAT: Waste Of Money, Breath And Time!

The sting in this trap is the sheer weight of pressure we are placing on ourselves to make the relationship work. To fall back on an old cliché, we are attempting to fit a round peg into a square hole.

In this kind of trap you become insular and dependent. Take time to check who or what you are running away from. The letting-go exercise in Chapter Four will help (see page 63).

6. the confessional trap

Here we go to the opposite extreme. We attempt to reveal everything to our partner, including all our sexual exploits with the fabled Tom, Dick and Harry. The hidden belief here is that if they know everything about us they cannot be shocked. 'What you see is what you get.' Unfortunately too much information too soon never helps to create a trusting partnership; new partners may fear us telling the world about their love life. Sharing special moments with every new conquest doesn't show a great deal of integrity.

In your journal, write down five things you may be trying to prove by being this way.

7. the sex trap

Have you ever tried the sex trap? This is where you try to become the sexiest person your partner has ever met. You literally bend over backwards to fulfil their sexual fantasies. The whole relationship is about *sex*. OK, truly, how long can you keep that up? (No innuendo meant.) A month? A year?

Sometimes people hide behind sex, interpreting good sex as love. 'If it feels good, it must be love.' This is not the truth. Love is from the heart and sex is just the plumbing. You will only attract compatible people when you show them who you really are, not what you can do.

Sometimes after the break up of a long-term relationship we may rebel and fall into this trap as a form of revenge, or just to prove that we are powerful. But in this trap sex is based on control and power and not on intimacy.

- Who is it that you are taking revenge on?
- Would you be willing to forgo the revenge in order to value yourself more?
- If you have ever behaved inappropriately and felt guilty, now is the time to let it go and forgive yourself. Life is too short to hold on to this guilt. See it all as another lesson you have learnt on your path back to heaven.

8. the fairytale trap

In this trap we expect our ideal partner to magically appear and sweep us off to live happily ever after. Of course, relationships rarely look like they do in romantic novels or films. If they did, disappointment would quickly set in, particularly when the partners that happen to jump into our lives act more like Kermit the frog than Prince Charming. Imaginary people fall in love quickly and live happily ever after on paper. Real people fall into love slowly and live fully ever after.

Make a list of how many frogs you have kissed. How many turned into princes? Do you really want to spend your nights washing someone's green tights and polishing their smelly codpiece? Time to wake up, princess, and write your own magical destiny.

9. the doormat trap

Here we ignore anything about our partner that does not fit into our expectations, values and lifestyle. We ignore behaviour that crosses our boundaries or hurts our feelings. We believe that there is a limited supply of possible partners, so we have to take what we can get or be alone. This results in relationship failure when we settle for less and compromise ourselves.

Remember the boundaries exercise from Chapter Four? You must be able to say 'no' to what you don't want in order to be available to say 'yes' to what you do. *You* have the power to choose who, what, where, when and how. You really can get what you want if you make effective choices aligned with your values.

What do you need from your partner to feel loved and nurtured? Start to communicate this to them so that they at least have an idea of what you want. The greatest problems I have witnessed in relationships stem from lack of communication.

10. the drama queen trap

Oh boy, do I know about this one! Drama after drama, crisis after crisis, never a peaceful moment. Everything has to have a huge emotional response. Some people use this strategy in order to establish a relationship. Their last partner may turn up unexpectedly and want them back, they may have ongoing family feuds that you get embroiled in or job losses, redundancy, unfair dismissal – anything to keep the drama going. The belief here is that every drama is a test to see if you are *meant* to be together through thick and thin.

The downfall here is that you always have to top the last crisis to keep them interested. If you don't have a drama going the relationship becomes boring, which is the worst nightmare of any Drama Queen worth her salt. But this level of drama cannot be sustained; it is emotionally draining for both parties.

Become aware of your drama patterns. It will help you understand that your partner's reaction may be less about you and more about their old heartbreaks. Keeping dramas going all the time prevents us from having to feel and be really honest about what is going on.

11. the praying mantis trap

This is when we pray for someone to come and rescue us, hoping a relationship will solve all our emotional and financial problems. Then we pray they will also bring happiness and fulfilment. We continually expect to be rescued by a hero or heroine and this will inevitably result in a sense of desperation, neediness and ultimately relationship failure.

To be in a successful relationship we should try to be in a position of having choice and being aware of our wants rather than just our neediness. If this is a particular problem you have, perhaps you could read the last chapter again, particularly the section on needs and neediness. No one can save you repeatedly. The knight or the hero who jumps in at the beginning of a relationship soon gets tired and resentments start to form, leading to resistance, rejection and revenge – all because you are not being accountable for your own life. The moment you do start to become accountable, how much more attractive you will become!

In your journal:

- List three needs you want your partner to fulfil.
- List three needs your partner would like fulfilled.
- List three needs you could fulfil yourself that you are currently expecting someone else to fulfil.

12. the calculator trap

Imagine strapping a great big calculator to the back of your partner and then strapping one onto your own back. When you go to hug each other, what you are really doing is pressing the imaginary calculator buttons where each of you keeps a tally of what you have brought into the relationship and what you believe you have received from the other. This is where you get into the trap of always negotiating – for time, love, chores, gifts – measuring your success against an economic yardstick of profit and loss.

Geraldine, a student of mine, said that she was happy to keep a pristine show house and to put up with her husband John's boorish behaviour as long as in return he gave her financial security. She knew that as long as she didn't rock the boat she could have a comfortable lifestyle, but the cost was enormous. She spent much of her time calculating – calculating his mood, calculating his finances, calculating his bonuses, and so on. On her credit side she'd calculate how many shirts she'd ironed that week and what slights she had endured in silence.

My advice to Geraldine was to learn to be authentic. She needed to stop giving just so she could get something in return and getting upset when it didn't 'equal' her gift. She needed to ask for what she wanted and needed, to develop the ability to say 'no' and to give unconditionally. That way the excitement could return to her life.

- Have you ever given solely to receive?
- How did you feel when it didn't match up to your expectations?
- Try giving without any expectations and see the difference. You will be pleasantly surprised.

☆ tricks and temptations

So much for the traps, now let's take a light-hearted look at some of the tricks and temptations we may play in our dating games. Tricks, traps and temptations are all distractions – they drain our energy. When we play dirty in the game of life we detract from our authentic self. These little cheating games are not just limited to the people we date or are in intimate relationships with; they leak into our workplace, friendships and families too.

the jealousy trick

Have you ever tried to make somebody jealous in order to make them take more notice of you? Jealousy is a very dangerous card to play; it can cause distrust throughout your relationship.

My friend used to send herself flowers as though they were from a mysterious admirer. She would act all surprised when they arrived and become all coy and shy when her boyfriend asked where they came from. It cost her a small fortune. Although it certainly got his attention, it wasn't long before it backfired. Whereas before her boyfriend had trusted her implicitly, now he is constantly checking where she is going and who she is seeing. Every man he meets in her company becomes the potential suitor.

Jealousy is based on insecurity. It acts like an umbrella hiding emotions including fear of abandonment, rejection and rage. There are many reasons why we feel jealous and although it is a normal human emotion, if we fail to tame it, it can get out of control. Jealousy can start a vicious circle of destructive feelings and can be all-consuming. It always leads to heartbreak.

the 'not available' trick

How about when you act like the life and soul of the party, pretending you have a hectic social life with the 'in' crowd – 'Only available between Ascot and Wimbledon, so book early' – when in fact you are sitting at home counting the seconds to the next date?

Felicity has played this card many times; it seemed to work for a while. However, any guy that lasted much beyond the trick soon found out that these friends in high places in fancy bars and restaurants were a figment of her imagination, fuelled through her reading of the latest gossip magazines. As part of her attraction was her imaginary lifestyle, the guys soon moved on.

Acting aloof and playing tricks will not help you to a happy social life.

the damsel in distress trick

This is a sure-fire way to capture the eye of a hero, knight or prince. They are all looking for someone to save. The trick here is to act all vulnerable like a fluffy chick with a broken wing who can't help herself, who can't change a plug or is in financial disarray. Damsels in distress have to give all their power away in order to trick somebody and if they maintain this role it is bound to all end in tears. When we start to show our true power, which eventually we all do, the hero/knight/prince doesn't know what to do. We become a threat to his role of helper. What happens when the hero/knight/prince wakes up and finds he's in bed with Boudecia or one of her warrior daughters? He's out of there like a cat out of hell. So be warned, don't waste your time dealing a hand like this to Mr Right.

temptations

Temptation comes in many forms, from status to sexy seduction to laundry services. The list is endless. But again, if we try to portray ourselves as something that deep down we are not, we won't be loved for ourselves and our needs won't be met.

The temptress is the woman everyone loves to hate: beautiful, sensual and sexual, She is every woman's worst nightmare and every man's favourite fantasy. Men adore her for the pleasure she provides. But they hate and fear her as well because her manipulative personality can expose their weaknesses.

Even in these supposedly enlightened times there are many temptresses out there. Nowadays we may tempt someone with our ability to help them in their business or may act as a therapist, healing all their hurts and listening to endless stories of woe. They think we care and at the beginning we probably do. Then the inevitable words come up: 'What about me?' and the tempted are amazed and shocked. They thought we had all the answers and now we are asking for something from them. Help!

All these forms of temptation lure in the unsuspecting just like the sirens of ancient Greek mythology, who played the flute and lyre and sang so sweetly they lured passing sailors to linger with them much longer than they should have. It is said that sirens were a threat because they gave men the choice of hearing about life instead of experiencing it.

Many classic books are also peopled with fabulous temptresses. In the Bible Eve and Delilah both tempted others and got their comeuppance. Eve was thrown out of Eden just for the sake of an apple and once Delilah got her hands on Samson's lock of hair she was no happier. Scarlett O'Hara in *Gone with the Wind* tried to tempt her beau with her southern charms. But when Rhett Butler discovered what she was really like, he uttered those famous words: 'Frankly, my dear, I don't give a damn.' In *Great Expectations* Estella is trained to be a temptress by Miss Haversham with the intent of breaking a poor boy's heart.

Temptresses may seem enticing, but by tempting others we are creating distance, disconnection and mistrust. Temptations are a form of manipulation designed to get us what we want and manipulation always backfires because it involves vampiring. And we can only tempt an unsuspecting partner for so long – the moment the truth is revealed, the relationship changes.

- In your journal, write down what type of tricks you have used in the past and how you may have tempted others. We sometimes feel bad about this afterwards. The guilt is itself a subtle trap to hold us back from being open and honest in future relationships. Make a 'guilty list' of all the tricks and temptations you have used. It is so freeing to clear our guilty memories from our hearts.
- When you have finished your list, sit for a while and read through it. Remember all those old places and times you felt guilty.
- Forgive yourself for these misunderstandings and then burn the list.

☆ manifesting romance

Have you ever noticed that when you are in a relationship or in love, there doesn't seem to be a scarcity of men or women who are attracted to you? When you are not in need of a partner, they are all over the place. It is your desperation and longing for your perfect mate that keeps them away. As you let go of the neediness, you will become more loving and start attracting potential partners like bees to honey – and you will find that person that makes your heart sing.

Once you have made the decision to move on, to step back onto the path of relationship, it is worth sitting and making a list of the qualities and gifts you would like to manifest in a partner. Making a 'manifesting list' is a way of decluttering your mind of all the feelings, needs, wants and desires that are spinning around your head about a partner.

The key gift here is to *relax* and to *breathe*. For me this exercise works best either last thing at night or first thing in the morning.

- Sit quietly for five minutes somewhere where you feel safe.
- Take in a deep breath and relax. In your mind's eye imagine a partner walking towards you.
- What do they look like?
- What do they sound like?
- Can you smell their freshness?
- How tall are they?
- What body shape do you prefer?
- What are all the qualities you want and admire in a partner?
- Spend some time visualizing this partner in every detail. Feel, hear, see, touch and taste them. Use all your senses to call them to you.
- As you visualize this partner, ask your Miracle Mind to include all the other qualities you require for true happiness.
- Relax, knowing everything you truly desire is on its way to you.

The key here is trust. Clients who trusted this exercise would work are now in relationships. The clients for whom it did not work all admitted that they doubted their power. This gives the universe conflicting messages; it is like saying that you are not ready to have your life's desires fulfilled. Doubts in your thinking create roadblocks along the path to finding your perfect mate. But when you let go of the need and your hungry eyes are relaxed, the universe gets to work on your behalf and *voilà*! So trust in your power and be specific about what you want.

Carly, an American woman I worked with, wrote a list of all the things she wanted in a relationship. Two weeks later she met a man who swept her off her feet. When she phoned to tell me what had happened she was excited, but there was a hesitation in her voice. I asked her what the problem was. She said that he was only five feet two inches tall and that his name was Wally. She had always preferred tall men and Wally was a name she had never liked! She hadn't been specific enough.

Another time, a friend living in Hawaii made the longest list you have ever seen to call in her mate. Again, within two weeks a fantastic partner manifested, but the biggest shock was that this partner was a woman! My friend hadn't put down what sex! Remember, *you get what you ask for, so be specific.*

Once you have listed everything you would like to manifest in a partner, it is also a good idea to list the gifts and qualities that you have to offer. Then you will be ready to step onto the path of relationship.

☆ the path of relationship

Although every relationship is unique they do tend to follow a certain path. I believe that there are six main steps along the path of relationship:

* romance
* honeymoon
* shadow figures
* power struggle
* zombie zone
* conscious relationship

Recognizing these stages and learning the lessons they contain could save you a whole lot of time and heartbreak.

romance

The first stage in a relationship is the romance. We meet, we think we like one another. We've been lonely for so long and now, finally(?), here's someone who understands us. We fall in love. We can't get enough of each other's company. We believe we've found the 'one and only', our 'soul mate'. The fairy stories are true! We have made it. There is a God.

At the beginning of a relationship the romance gives us a taste of everything the relationship can be. We start living in a Technicolor world. Life is so bright we have to don 'love goggles'. We experience all the fun, beauty and passion of relationship. Nature quickly takes over here; when people say, 'We have chemistry,' it is actually nature setting up a form of anaesthetic to numb the brain and heighten all the other senses. This allows a couple to get close enough for long enough to create babies; chemistry is a serum that ensures the survival of the species. But it works equally well for those not contemplating having children. The serum still kicks in. It doesn't take into account age, sex or sexual persuasion.

With romance and nature's anaesthetic working in cahoots we find we can't breathe without our mate; we feel good all over; the smallest joke makes us laugh. There is a spring in our step and our bodies feel different (that's the anaesthetic). We enter the 'me too' period here. It sounds like this:

* 'I would love to live near the sea one day.' *'Me too.'*
* 'I've always wanted to go trekking.' *'Me too.'*
* 'I love cricket, rugby, golf, opera, dancing.' *'Me too.'*
* 'I adore double chocolate-chip dairy ice cream.' *'Me too.'*
* 'I would love to drop out of the rat race and raise ostriches.' *'Me too.'*

We just can't get enough of each other. This is 'tanga time', when we buy sexy underwear and have great sex. We preen and take care of ourselves more than ever before, just in case there is the opportunity for a passionate embrace.

honeymoon

The romance and honeymoon stages tend to blend into each other. Honeymoon is all about anticipation. For most couples there is a noticeable change in the relationship about the time they make a definite commitment to each other. Once they say, 'Let's set up home...' 'Why not move in?' 'Two can live as cheaply as one' or 'Let's get married', the romance has become more serious. This is where we want to show the world we can make it, we are a couple, we won't make the mistakes others have made and we are different: 'It's you and me against the world.' When in fact the 'world' is looking on and saying 'Good luck!'

shadow figures

The honeymoon period is over once the anticipation turns into expectation and demands. We begin to know each other well enough to notice the flaws. The anaesthetic wears off. The love goggles that have blinded us fall away. All our partner's quirky and annoying ways become all too visible. The relationship that we believed was made in heaven becomes more like the film *Nightmare on Elm Street* and our partner becomes Freddy Kruger – the embodiment of everything we didn't want in a relationship. This is a sign that the hidden beliefs we have about men/women/relationships are coming back to be healed.

Old hurts are reactivated as we realize that our partners cannot or will not love and care for us as they promised. Our dream shatters. We become critical of everything that we previously professed to love. At this stage we project all the unhealed parts onto our partner. The nice, sweet, good girl or charming prince has gone. The shadow figure is here. You wake up to find yourself in bed with your worst nightmare. How did this happen?

Always remember that *every relationship goes through this stage*. None of us is perfect – who would want to *have* to be? – and we all carry our rackets with us. This is the point when we begin to use them. (Not all fights are obvious – some people would rather die than fight, but their silences can be deafening.) We sometimes think it's all over and we would never want to repeat that drama, yet we remember the romance and honeymoon and want to try again. For some couples this becomes a form of foreplay. For others this could be the end of the relationship. There is an alternative, which is to choose to see every shadow stage as an opportunity to heal past hurts. Recommitting to your partner here strengthens your relationship, taking you back to the romance and honeymoon stages.

Understanding where you are in this cycle will help you to move forward. I never said the path of relationship was an easy one, yet the rewards are well worth the effort.

power struggle

One step on from the shadow figures and here the rackets are out big time, though it's not always obvious. This is where we often use words of endearment with a sarcastic undertone. 'Darling, please take the bins out.' 'Sweetie, don't touch me there.' And a simple 'Yes, dear' can take on a whole new meaning.

There is an amazing book by Dan Greenburg and Suzanne O'Malley called *How to Avoid Love and Marriage*, which gives a tongue-in-cheek description of how sarcasm and mimicking can undermine a relationship. When I first read this it was a revelation; I could identify exactly what I had been doing in my past relationships. In it they describe something very similar to what I term 'the power-struggle stance'.

Try this and see if it fits your stance when you are ready for a tiff. Stand with your hands on hips, head to one side, nodding your head, shoulders totally stiff. At the same time imagine you are sucking a lemon and have a nasty smell under your nose that stops you from breathing normally.

With the power-struggle stance, you will find your voice may rise two octaves above that of your mate. You will start to mimic anything they say, accenting and drawing out every second or third syllable that you see as self-important or self-pitying. It is all a far cry from the romance stage when we just loved and lusted, when every little joke made us laugh.

At this most unsettling time we can also gain a 'psychic ability'. We can become mind-readers overnight. We pride ourselves on knowing our partner's every need. We assume that we know them inside out. We also assume that they understand our every desire, our every need, our every sigh, our every wish. But how can anybody do that? It's impossible. When we start mind-reading, we are actually controlling the situation. We are really saying: 'You are not capable of taking care of yourself.' I can hear some of you saying, 'But they *can't*!' Oh yes, they can! They managed before and they will manage again, on their own if needs be.

Communication is the most important factor in a successful relationship. When you are mind-reading, your partner will not appreciate you one bit and the relationship is doomed for failure. Before assuming what they want, check with them. Explain what your needs are. Relationships change all the time, and so do your needs. If you learn to communicate regularly, it will save much misunderstanding and heartbreak. Don't assume your partner knows your every need, wish, expectation. They aren't psychic either.

How well do you know your partner? After realizing that your crystal ball and mind-reading don't work, answer these questions. If you don't know the answer, find out. Get to know them again. One of the most important features of successful couples is the quality of their communication. Do you know your partner's inner world? Do they know yours?

- Can you name your partner's best friends?
- Do you know three things they tolerate about you?
- Do you know what their life goals are?
- Do you know what they value about the relationship?
- Do you know what stresses your partner is currently facing?
- Do you think your partner knows you pretty well?
- Is there fire and passion in the relationship on both sides?
- Do you appreciate the things they do in this relationship?
- At the end of the day are you both glad to see each other?
- Is your partner your best friend?
- Do you really listen to their complaints?

This isn't a quiz, it is just designed to give you some idea where you could improve your communication with your mate. Have they become your mat or are they still your mate? There will probably be strengths you can build upon and maybe some weak spots that need some of your attention. Ask your partner to do this quiz and then discuss your findings. Make it a special evening together on your own – you never know, it could lead back to the romance stage for you both.

During the power-struggle stage we are not trying to communicate as much as to score points off our opponent (sorry, slip of the tongue, I mean partner!) The 'me toos' of the romance turn into 'don't want tos'. We begin to complain about our partner's driving, jokes, friends and their family. The tanga knickers are stuffed to the back of the top drawer and out come the comfy knickers – you know the ones. That little sexy negligee magically changes into a wyncyette nightie with matching bedsocks or an old sloppy T-shirt from last year's holiday. His sexy Calvin Klein boxer shorts become washed-out grey saggy Y-fronts. How did this happen?

In any relationship, partners polarize. It is similar to the positive and negative terminals on a battery – both terminals are needed to create a circuit. We all have a negative and a positive force in the relationship. Although we act differently, we are feeling the same on the inside. Next time you are in a fight, remember you are both trying to get your needs met with your old style of manipulation.

The gift you need to heal this power-struggle stage is to talk, talk, talk. Talk about the issues that aren't working in the relationship. Talk about your needs. Talk about your dreams. Talk about what is not working for you, with no blame or judgement attached. I know this can be hard, but good relationships are worth working for. Relationships are like puppies; they need loving, nurturing, watering and taking out occasionally. (And yes, sometimes you have to clear the mess up with a pooper-scooper.)

When you and your partner actually start to understand the path of relationship and what is happening to you both and how normal it is, you can transform any negative situations easily and diplomatically. Recognize each other's gifts. When the problem-finder acknowledges the problem-solver and starts to respect their position, the couple can make a great team. The negative partner can get in touch with the problems and the positive partner can transform them. It is important to note that we can be the negative force in some areas and the positive in others.

What we need to understand and accept is that conflict is supposed to happen. As spiritual amnesia fades and we start to remember why we came to the planet, we realize that conflict is only a sign. It is showing us all the fractured places in our heart so that we can heal them and become whole. So why not have some fun while you are doing it?

This exercise is all about healing the power struggle. Now we have looked at all the negative stuff, let's look at how we can make it all work. What identifies a good relationship to you? Unbelievably, most of these steps are simple and remarkably easy to implement. Why not try it and see what happens?

S.O.S. – seek outside support.

According to a recent report, the average time a couple in distress waits before first seeking outside help is six years, and that half of the relationships that end do so in the first seven years. So if you need help, find it, and quick. Don't wait! False pride has no place in a relationship.

say what you mean without saying it mean

When you start to feel any anger coming up, do not blame the other person. Feel where your anger is coming from, take responsibility, be accountable. I can assure you that every emotion will have a story attached to it. Talk it through with your partner; you will only get closer by dropping the roles and showing your authentic self.

count to ten

This may be an old remedy, but it's a sure-fire winner. One of the litmus tests of the state of a marriage is how quickly an argument starts up. Sometimes we are just waiting for the 'one and only' to say 'just one more word' before we are ready to bite their heads off. Maybe you feel like Clint Eastwood in *Dirty Harry* with his Magnum 45. In your mind you are saying, 'Go on, make my day ...' If this is going on at any time in your life, just *breathe* and count to ten.

do the partnership dance

A relationship succeeds to the extent that you are both willing to understand and be influenced by each other's points of view. This means accepting and acknowledging each other's strengths and weaknesses, allowing one to lead and the other to follow but always being willing to change position. It's about listening in order to understand, speaking in order to be understood.

define boundaries

Having clear boundaries is essential to a healthy, growing partnership. Boundaries are one of the keys to an intimate relationship and affect every area of our lives. (Revisit Chapter Four on boundaries and values if you have particular problems in this area.)

bring in a 'breaking state'

Whenever you are having a heated discussion, a fight or a difference of opinion that is starting to escalate, set up a signal with your partner (possibly from a favourite comedy show or movie) that either of you can use to interrupt the pattern of an argument. This will give you both a chance to re-evaluate the importance of what it is you are arguing about. Try something as silly as 'Can I smell bacon burning?' The mind has to stop and smell to see if there is anything burning. Laughter can free you. It is impossible to laugh and be angry at the same time. Try it!

think in terms of karmic banking

Imagine having a bank account in heaven where every positive act gives you a credit and every negative act is a debit – an 'emotional bank account'. Happy relationships are happy at least in part because both people's accounts are in credit.

Find out from your partner what they think would constitute a deposit. For example, what is it they are always giving you? Do they go and get the Sunday papers and bring you a cup of tea in the morning? Do they surprise you with presents or buy funny little cards to say the words they wish they could say to you? Do they organize a surprise night out? Maybe you could surprise them for once.

Then think about what constitutes a debit (getting home late, working weekends when you've planned something, a forgotten birthday). Generally, seek to make at least five credits for every debit you contribute to the account and be aware that if things haven't been going well for a while it may take some time for you to pay off your emotional overdraft!

the zombie zone

In the power-struggle stage we often decide that we are right and the other person is wrong. We become judge, jury and jailer, but what we don't realize is that we've also locked ourselves into a jail sentence with them and that could mean 20 years or more in the dreaded 'zombie zone'.

The zombie zone is when we disconnect from our dreams, defend our roles and divorce becomes an option. All of these are a sure sign that we are walking in the land of the living dead. Terminal boredom has taken root. We are bored because we've disconnected emotionally; we have been defending our roles to make ourselves right. If you insist on being right all the time, you become righteous, and the righteous role causes you to become disillusioned with your life and partner.

In the zombie zone neither partner is willing to give to the other what they need. They no longer see or care much about each other. In the last stage of the power struggle we could manipulate situations in order to get our needs met by tantrums, crying, withdrawal and criticism – anything to get a reaction. But in the zombie zone even this doesn't work. There is a deadness. We are stuck and tired, and we feel we have been sacrificing forever. Have you ever seen couples out for a so-called 'celebratory dinner' hardly speaking a word to each other all night? We may settle into an uneasy truce for years, or seek help out of this impasse. Divorce is the last step. We think another partner will help us feel alive and whole again. And they may, for a short while. However, what isn't healed in one relationship will come up again in the next. The whole cycle will start again, only this time with a newer model.

The way out of this impasse is bonding, fun and intimacy. You can make a monumental choice here to move the partnership forward. You can choose your partner all over again. You can commit to the relationship again. You know your partner intimately and all their flaws. Would you be willing to join them again, to allow the gift of forgiveness to heal the old pain?

Ask yourself whether you want to be dead right now or you want to be happy. You can choose to be present, to listen, to make time for a truer contact with your partner. You can choose to give more time, give more love and give more appreciation. The more you give, the more you will know who you truly are. When you feel you have nothing left to give, ask for heaven's help. The helpers in heaven are waiting to give you all the love you need to move you and your relationship back into the flow. Try the following exercise.

Breathe deeply, take a moment to close your eyes, and imagine the universe pouring down all kinds of energy and light. As you are filled with this energy, feel how you are motivated to give, especially to your partner.

- What is the simple thing they need? The simplest of things can show your love. Life is meant to be simple, although the Ego Dramatist tells us differently.
- When was the last time you connected up to your Miracle Mind and received help?
- What is the gift in your Spiritual Backpack that you have always wanted to receive from your partner? Would it be appreciation, acknowledgement, love?
- Imagine them standing in front of you and giving you this gift at last.
- How do you feel?

When you have joined with your partner again and committed to the relationship you will have stepped through into a new kind of relationship. This is a freer relationship, a conscious relationship. It is the relationship of the future.

conscious relationships

The relationship of the future is actually already here. I see many couples who have gone through each of these steps on the path of relationship and decided to choose and commit to their partner – again! This time the partnership is at a higher level.

This stage does not come after a few short months; typically, it takes years to get here. This is the pay-off phase. Seeing your partner again, this time with all the qualities you admire, can be quite a revelation. You fall in love again. Love has been tempered in the heat of the power struggle and weathered all the storms.

These partners are on the same team. When they feel safe enough to be authentic, the illusions fade and they rediscover the real person. Nature's tricks have worked: the passion that was ignited at first sight has hurled two people into the drama of a shaky relationship and then developed into a bonded partnership. After all the tricks nature has played – anaesthetic, blindness and amnesia – this turns out to be a success story. This couple becomes interdependent; they support each other's growth and encourage each other to do what they love. Theirs is a love that accepts unconditionally. They both still have their own power and express themselves spontaneously and creatively, but they also now respond to the real needs of their partner. They grow beyond self-interest to exchange the love they both need. No words, thoughts or feelings are left unexpressed. Theirs is a love that will endure through time, and through which both will evolve. This is the goal for all relationships.

As soon as we have reached a level of maturity we will have relationships of quality and spirit. We will be able to love unconditionally and choose to connect to the spirit and light within, not just the outer form. With help from your Miracle Mind always available, you can transform your life. Your relationship can make it from the romance stage to the conscious stage without falling into the zombie zone!

Good luck on your path of relationship.

☆ healerette's happy hour

Here are some fun things to do with your partner. If these don't appeal I'm sure you can think of many others in a similar spirit. Use your imagination!

* Go to the park and play Cathy and Heathcliff.
* Meet in a bar and pretend it's the first time you have met and it's lust at first sight.
* Hide under the bedclothes and tell each other ghost stories.
* Find out what your partner's favourite toy was as a child and buy them one for Christmas.

Here are some you could also do with your friends:

* Spend a day at the seaside with buckets and spades (and coats and scarves).
* Go to the fun fair and try all the rides.
* Buy a kite and go kite flying.
* Sing opera – especially if you can't sing!

Chapter Six

success

Success is to laugh often and much
To win the respect of people and the affection of children
To earn the appreciation of honest critics and endure the betrayal of false friends
To appreciate beauty
To find the best in others
To leave the world a better place
To know everyone you loved has breathed easier because you have lived
This is to have succeeded.

ANON

Success is who you are, not what you do or what you have. It's internal. It's about what matters to *you*. External success is connected to performance, competition and attachment. External performances come and go. Success, like happiness, has to come from the inside. It is all about value and motivation. These are yours, not anyone else's. So this chapter is not just about career success, lifestyle success, relationship success; it is about success in areas you may have only ever dreamt about. It will help you to define what is really important to you and show you how to turn stumbling blocks into stepping-stones to success.

One thing that I find very reassuring is that we are all successful human beings just the way we are. If we never did another thing in our life, we would still be intrinsically successful. Here is a well-kept secret: we are made up from one egg and one sperm. No, it's not a biology lesson. Before conception we didn't physically exist, we were a consciousness waiting to be invited onto planet earth. As the egg and the sperm joined, we started on our physical journey. Before that the sperm had one hell of a journey trying to get to the much-prized egg. That little sperm was one of millions trying to be successful. Its journey would be equivalent to swimming from Britain across the Atlantic to the USA, tap-dancing across each state in the USA and then still having enough energy to pierce the barricaded precious castle wall that protected the golden egg that is the other half of you. *That is success!* You made it here.

snakes and ladders

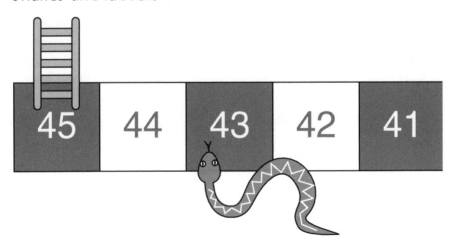

When we played the game snakes and ladders as children, we had to throw a double six to get started. I remember how I would close my eyes really tight and scrunch up my face. I had a belief that if I put enough of my energy into the wish it would happen. I would whisper, 'Double six, double six, double six,' and wouldn't open my eyes until the very last second. Focusing on the double six, as the dice left my hand I let go of the need to have the double six. I didn't get upset if it didn't magically appear – I knew I had done everything in my power to help. As children, our lighthearted attitudes meant that the game was more about fun and laughter than about winning. We all had our own special strategies for getting the right numbers. One friend quietly prayed and promised to be good for a week if she could just get a double six to start, another had a lucky charm. It didn't matter what we did to get that double six, what mattered was that we all trusted that everything would be alright in the end. We were grateful for our little community, our friendships and the simple pleasure of playing the game just for fun.

As children we knew it didn't really matter who started first on the board. We knew that in snakes and ladders one minute you could be at the top of the ladder and nearly winning and with the next throw of the dice you'd be sliding down the snake back to where you started. If we lost, we didn't dwell on our unsuccessful strategies, our unanswered prayers and the failure of our lucky charms. Snakes and ladders taught me that all I needed to play well was to have a sense of wonder and enthusiasm, and to know the game was all about participating, trusting and not being frightened of starting all over again. One of the High-Heeled Healer's key mantras is: 'Life doesn't have to be a battle, it can be a game.'

When we play games as children we are actually being taught many life skills. Unfortunately, just as we get spiritual amnesia and forget why we are here, so we forget these powerful secrets of success. In this chapter, we will take steps to regain some of that innocent enthusiasm. We will learn how to choose the ladders that lead to success and how to avoid the snakes that sabotage success.

Throughout this book we have discussed how our hidden beliefs, roles, patterns, competitiveness, judgements and guilt block us from passion and adventure. These are just a few of our sabotage snakes. We can also add jealousy, revenge and regrets, not to mention the 'f' words: fear and failure. By learning to avoid these snakes and choosing to climb the ladders of success we can move at the speed of light towards our aspirations.

Remember that this game of snakes and ladders does not depend on the roll of the dice, but on our choices.

☆ what does success really mean for you?

Everyone wants success but what one person terms success may not be true for another. To create success you must first define what is important to *you*. Don't be swayed by the media or the latest fad. Don't listen to the spin doctors or the fashion gurus. I do not want you to give your mother's, your partner's, or your boss's definition.

The more I thought about this, the more I realized that the secret wasn't just about having a definition, but about how you *know* you are successful at any given moment in time.

Using a few powerful words, state how you know you are successful.

- I know I am successful when I ...
- I know I am successful when I ...
- I know I am successful when I ...
- I know I am successful when I ...

One of my clients, Stacey, had changed her career two years previously from an executive in a computer firm to a life coach working successfully from her home office. In answer to these questions she wrote:

- 'I know I am successful when a client rings to renew a contract.'
- 'I know I am successful when I hear laughter in my home.'
- 'I know I am successful when I don't worry about money.'
- 'I know I am successful when I can run up the stairs and not be out of breath.'

Stacey's answers neatly covered the four main areas in her life: career, relationships, wealth and health. She could check in easily to feel, hear and know that she was successful at any time.

These are such universal areas to want to be successful in that it is worth repeating this exercise for each area:

Relationship:
- I know I am successful when I …
- I know I am successful when I …

Career:
- I know I am successful when I …
- I know I am successful when I …

Wealth:
- I know I am successful when I …
- I know I am successful when I …

Health:
- I know I am successful when I …
- I know I am successful when I …

Here are some answers from other clients:
- 'I know I am successful when I am respected by others.'
- 'I know I am successful when I am doing the work I love.'
- 'I know I am successful when I look back on my achievements and enjoy them all over again.'
- 'I know I am successful when I look at my reflection and have a clear conscience.'
- 'I know I am successful when the people around me treat me with respect and equality of heart.'

Do this exercise again and again and you will find out what's important to you. That is success. The exercise will unconsciously move you to a more peaceful place and the information will help you define the things that make you feel successful. You may even start to design a completely new life to fit in with these definitions. This could be the most important exercise in your life!

That's quite a heavy thought, so here's a wonderful visualization you can do to lighten up:

- Relax.
- Take a deep breath.
- Imagine what it would feel like if you knew what success truly felt like.
- How would it feel to you?
- What would you see?
- What would you hear people saying?
- Who would be with you?
- Stay there a while, enjoy the sensation. Visualize success.

There's only one corner of the universe you can be certain of improving, and that is your own self.
ALDOUS HUXLEY

☆ the success sabotage snakes

Now you have a better idea of what constitutes success for you, you can find out which sabotaging snakes are causing you to fail. The seven most common saboteurs are fear, guilt, revenge, jealousy, gossip, worry and regrets.

fear

When I researched the dynamics of blocks to success, I realized that the deepest root of any problem was the dreaded 'f' word: fear. But fear of failure or fear of success?

Several years ago, I worked on the reservations in northern BC, Canada, with my good friend Edna Brillon from the Haida tribe in the Queen Charlotte Islands. I was welcomed with so much love and curiosity. Although I am British I have a dark complexion, so it came as no surprise to me that people presumed I belonged to another tribe. They asked me which one. With my tongue firmly in my cheek I told them I came from the 'Eee by gum' tribe and our war cry was 'Ecky thump!'

When they realized I was from Manchester, all I heard was: 'David Beckham, Georgie Best, Matt Busby', all successful heroes in the football world. Sport, which is all about excellence and success, is a great way to make contact with the young and not so young.

I asked how many of the group had felt successful in their lives. Nobody would put their hand up and admit to being successful. They all sat there, too embarrassed to say in front of their friends and family that they had any success in their lives.

My next question was: 'OK, who has ever felt a failure?' Every hand shot up amidst great merriment. Everybody was happy to own up to feeling a failure. I then told them jokingly, 'Well, that makes you all very successful at being failures, doesn't it?' And yet these wonderful, loving, creative people were some of the most successful people I have ever had the privilege of working with. They were just very, very shy of their success. This is a normal reaction; I have seen it all around the world, in all walks of life.

Consider what would happen if you were to be very successful.

- What would you have to do?
- What wouldn't you have to do?
- Who would you have to be?

- What negative effects would success bring? (Maybe fears of vitality vampires, energy thieves, gold diggers and so on.)
- What are your fears about your success?
- By not being successful what are you proving and to whom?
- Who is it you feel separate from now?
- Imagine creating a rainbow bridge to them, creating a bond, healing any separation and allowing success to flow through you to them.
- Give them the gift of success.

Whatever you have a fear of, you also have an attraction to. All the times we have said to ourselves 'I want success', our Ego Dramatist has been playing the blockbuster movie of our 'life as a failure' inside our heads. Why does this happen? Use the next exercise to examine your attraction to failure.

In your journal, write a short story about why you are a total failure ... This may be a hard exercise but have some fun with it. Make it the juiciest, most awful life you can imagine. How against all the odds and no matter how hard you tried, success eluded you. How at every turn there were bandits and bounders stopping your every strategy. Once you get this story into the open you can let it go once and for all.

guilt

Guilt is the superglue of life, it's what keeps us stuck, it's what we have used to make an altar to perhaps just one or two mistakes we made years ago. We pay homage to those mistakes daily by being a failure in our own eyes. Not anybody else's eyes, just ours. The whole world could look at us and see success. But inside, we will be feeling like frauds and failures, playing small and working hard to pay the guilt off.

We experience guilt when we use someone or something to hold ourselves back. Making the choice to let go of this and use the gifts of accountability and choice will move us forward in our life.

Greg, a lovely man in his fifties, retired early through ill-health and a redundancy payment he couldn't refuse. He attended a workshop in London, where he had lived all his life. He said that he constantly felt guilty and now that he had the time and the money he wanted to get to the bottom of this slimy sabotage snake and step into a new way of living. I suggested maybe we could market a new deodorant called 'Guilt Free'. All you would have to do when you felt guilty would be to spray yourself with it and off you'd go, straight back to innocence. Greg laughed, imagining himself on a market stall in the East End shouting 'Guilt free, guilt free, come an' get yer guilt free!'

Greg said he felt guilty about his ex-wife, whom he had left years ago for a younger woman. When he left her and the children he hadn't been thinking straight and now he was sorry to think he could have been so selfish. I asked him how he was paying for this guilt, as guilt always has a heavy price tag attached to it. He thought for a moment, then looked surprised and said, 'With my health.' 'So you have ill-health to pay back the guilt?' 'Yep, I've beaten myself up so much to make her feel sorry for me.' 'Is this a successful strategy? Does she feel sorry for you?' 'Actually, she remarried a few years after I left to a good man who took my kids on and apparently she is very happy. She has said to my kids many a time how she wishes me well.' 'So your plan hasn't really worked, has it?'

I asked Greg if that day he would be willing to let go of the guilt he'd been carrying around and choose health instead as the gift hidden behind it. He took a deep breath and with a sparkle in his eye said it was time for him to get on with his life and have a relationship again. He wanted his health back and to meet his kids and ex and clear any misunderstandings at last.

As Greg let go of his self-imposed burden of guilt his health improved dramatically. He moved to the coast, started a small business and is now happily dating again. That is success.

The Ego Dramatist will trick us into beating ourselves up in many, many ways in order to pay off the guilt we feel. Take some time to answer these questions in your journal:

- What are you still feeling guilty about?
- How are you using guilt to hold yourself back?
- Can you choose to receive the gift of success instead?
- You have the maturity and the wisdom to do that now! Are you willing?

revenge

How many times do you complain about what is missing in your life? Do you feel it's someone else's fault? The hidden dynamic in revenge is that we are getting back at a significant other, often a parent or partner we feel has let us down. When we fail, we are subconsciously sending out the message: 'I am not successful because of you.'

Revenge stories abound in relationships; there are books about how to get revenge, films about revenge, and so on. *The First Wives Club* was a comedy about three friends who were all dumped by their partners. They decided to get revenge by being more successful than their exes, using some sneaky tricks along the way. However, they didn't feel that great once they'd had their revenge. Revenge is a block to success. No matter how successful we may seem to the outside world, if we feel the need for revenge we are holding on to resentment, which can only embitter our lives.

Revenge is a double-edged sword: as you lift it high above your head you are in danger of hurting both yourself and another. As we take our revenge on others, it is always true that we are getting revenge on ourselves as well.

Ask yourself:

- By not being successful, who is it I'm taking revenge on?
- Close your eyes and imagine this person standing in front of you.
- Is the fight with them worth more than your success?
- Give them the gift of success. As you do, you will feel yourself being filled with peace and relaxation.

jealousy

The green-eyed monster of jealousy can play havoc with your life. Jealousy is like an umbrella covering many other negative emotions such as hurt, unworthiness, anger and possessiveness. When we feel jealous, many old memories surface and we feel as though we are swimming in a sea of emotions. To try and stop these feelings we may take on the roles of high moralist or super-snoop detective. How many times have you been jealous and gone through your partner's pockets? Their e-mails? Address book? We start looking for something to incriminate them with… Columbo will be lucky to hang on to his detective job when we get the 'jealousy umbrella' out.

This particular sabotage snake is normally ignored by society – who would want to own up to all that emotion? I sometimes think I will start 'Jeal-Anon', a 12-step programme for when you get stuck in the jealousy jam.

Jessica, a nursing sister at a local hospital, complained that she spent her life working and looking after her patients as well as doing all the household chores whilst her partner of 15 years, Kyle, came home from the office, showered and went to play pool with his buddies four nights a week. Jessica wasn't jealous of another woman, but of Kyle's freedom and friendships. She agreed that the way forward was to discuss her feelings with him.

During this discussion it became clear that Kyle was also jealous. He was jealous of Jessica's career, seeing her as having an interesting, varied day meeting lots of people while he went to the same boring dead-end job in the same boring office and met the same boring people week in and week out. Jessica was shocked: she never knew that Kyle was unhappy in his job. The outcome of their talk was that Jessica was to cut down her shifts and share more of the housework with Kyle. This gave them time and energy to deepen their relationship and to research options for a future business together. Remember, in any kind of fight the other person is probably feeling exactly the same, just acting differently.

If you feel jealous for any reason you are probably listening to your Ego Dramatist, who believes your world is fuelled by lack. This is not a good place to be. Do you know what emotions are under your 'jealousy umbrella'? Try this exercise:

- When was the first time you remember feeling jealous?
- Who were you jealous of?
- What was going on at the time?
- What were you jealous about?
- How did you show your jealousy?
- On a scale from one to ten, how much energy do you still have running about that experience?
- Today, can you let go of any energy or jealousy you have attached to that situation or person?
- Imagine seeing the person in your mind's eye and knowing that you live in an abundant world. Give them one of your special gifts from your Spiritual Backpack. See the surprise on their face and feel the power of giving unconditionally.

When feelings of jealousy come up, repeat the words: 'These feelings are keeping me from success.' The negative energy attached to jealousy will begin to dissolve as you keep repeating this mantra.

gossip

Do you talk about other people behind their backs? Do you put people down or criticize their every move? Gossip has ruined lives, split families, alienated friends. Once it's out there, it cannot be taken back. The words harm, maim and sometimes even kill. Spreading rumours, tittle-tattle, back-biting quips, looks that can kill and cursing – these are all forms of gossiping. The world media lives in a feeding frenzy of gossip and it has become part of our culture. I have been on both sides of the fence. I have gossiped about others and been gossiped about, and from both perspectives it is damaging to your success, happiness and energy.

The main thing to remember here, using your gifts of accountability and choice, is that what you see in others and gossip about is what you don't particularly like about yourself. If you notice and talk about other people's faults, they're very probably yours.

Contrary to popular belief, putting others down doesn't make them smaller; it makes you look petty, unkind and even vindictive. Instead of the negative spiky arrows leaving your heart, how about some good old-fashioned blessings? Find some positive traits about that person, acknowledge yourself for having the same quality and free yourself from all those barbed words returning to your heart. Remember this rhyme: 'When you blame, you maim.' You are hurting two people – yourself and another. You simply cannot attack another person without distorting your own energy in a negative way and drawing the consequences of that into your life.

If there is a problem, acknowledge it and ask: 'What's the solution?' Come up with a new approach, even if you have to go in search of it. If you do this, your life will become an adventure, rather than a chore, and you will create new opportunities.

If you can, be supportive of people's good qualities and ignore the bad. If you can't do that, give the people you don't like plenty of space and go your own way. Your lack of attention will disconnect them from you, and make you more attractive to people who mirror your better qualities.

Realize that every person you meet is a teacher and has a gift or message for you. If you are constantly critical, you are losing a fabulous opportunity to receive that gift or message and move ahead in your own growth.

Look for the best in others and you will grow into a giant. Look for the worst in others and you will shrink. As you break the gossip habit, wonderful things happen. Relationships are healed, self-respect is enhanced and success has a safe place to visit.

■ Think of a person you have gossiped about.
■ Can you list five good qualities that you see in them?

- How are you similar to them?
- Next time you think of that person, send them some blessings. You will receive them back tenfold.

worry

Everyone worries, but have you noticed that most of the things you worry about never happen? I used to believe that if I worried about a problem, I was keeping it at bay. I felt if I was constantly on my guard, my worst worries would disappear. It never worked – all that happened was that I was so shattered the next morning through lack of sleep I would then worry about how exhausted I looked or something equally as trivial. Now that is totally insane. To deal with worries successfully, we need to develop resilience and the ability to bounce back.

Make a worry bank. Find a box or a container and customize it, so you can keep it by your bed. Make an opening that looks like a letter box and every night before you go to sleep, write down on a piece of paper what your top three worries are. You will sleep more soundly and your worries always look different in the morning.

Remember, today is the tomorrow you worried about yesterday. Was it worth it?

regrets

Many of us think back to idyllic times in the past when we felt that we were happier, more successful, more fulfilled, and so on. Thinking back to those times is just a way of making up for the lack our Ego Dramatist feels right now. Living on past successes doesn't allow us to move towards a more exciting future.

Living in a museum full of relics, replaying idyllic times, is really a lie. Because even during those times, there was undoubtedly something missing that drove us on to search for something more. Stop harkening back to the past and start to let go of all the sentences beginning with 'if only …' 'If only …' is robbing you of the past and the future.

Choose to let go of the past and value yourself right now by working through this exercise:

- Consciously choose to be present, bringing all the energy that has been stuck in past regrets inside you now.
- Imagine that all the joy and happiness in the world is filling you up right now.
- What colour would it be?
- What kind of lovely feeling is there?
- Let this fill every part of you: your toes, feet, ankles, legs, body, heart, lungs, all your organs, your arms, neck, face, head, eyes, ears and the very crown of your head. Feel it overflowing.

Success is within you and a natural part of you.

☆ the seven steps to success

Have you ever reached the top of the ladder of success only to find it was leaning against the wrong wall? These seven steps to success will ensure that you are leaning the ladder in the right place because you will be focusing on *your own inner success*. Free from the need to prove yourself to others, you will be able to enjoy your success to the full. Wherever you are, whatever you are doing, whoever you are with, you will feel successful. Remember, success is an inside job.

These seven steps can be used in any area where you are searching for success. Try them, and choose to be a success in your own eyes.

1. humour

There are three things which are real: God, human folly and laughter.
The first two are beyond our comprehension. So we must do what we can with
the third.
JOHN F. KENNEDY

Step one on the ladder of success is humour. Your worth is not determined by your successes or failures. Keep in mind that *you* are not *your blunders.* Learn to laugh at your slip-ups and accept your weak spots. By developing your ability to accept your mistakes and laugh about them you are freeing up your energy to feel success.

taking humour seriously

Humour helps you to keep your head clear when you're dealing with difficult situations. It's a very powerful way to open doors, minds and hearts. Humour can save you time, money and pain and has the added benefit of keeping you healthy and stress-free. Norman Cousins' bestselling book *Anatomy of an Illness* explains that laughter is like 'internal jogging'. It enhances the respiration and circulation, oxygenates the blood, suppresses the stress-related hormones in the brain and activates the immune systems. Indeed, laughter is a gift we are all born with. It is a universal language; there are no accents or dialects. It is a great leveller.

Humour and laughter in organizations can increase the amount of feedback you can get, the honesty and the capacity for people to tell you good things. All the solutions to problems in organizations are within your own people, but the problem is that half of them don't want to say anything because they usually get zapped. It's through humour that you can open up the lines to communication.
KEN BLANCHARD, AUTHOR OF *THE ONE-MINUTE MANAGER*

The bottom line is that humour can be an effective way of building positive working relationships which then lead to success all round because humour and creativity go hand in hand. I believe that healing should be a loving, creative, humorous human interchange. When I'm teaching we all laugh and sometimes cry at the same time, clearing and lightening our hearts. It's amazing how transformational laughter can be.

Laughter, love, trust, faith, hope and the willingness to truly live are all we need to be healthy and successful human beings. If our only reasons for being on this planet are happiness and healing, humour definitely is the best recipe for success.

There are thousands of ways to invite smiles and laughter into your life. You don't have to be a stand-up comic or make a fool of yourself to raise a laugh. Here are some tips on how to get more 'smileage' out of your life:

- What are your favourite one-liners? One-liners pack a powerful one-two punch of wit and wisdom into a short sentence. They say something in a funny, potent and memorable way. What are your favourites?
- Tell some funny stories about yourself. The ability to laugh at yourself is incredibly freeing. List some of the excuses you have used over the years – excuses for being late, ill or absent – or list your most embarrassing moments.
- Who makes you laugh the most? What is it about that person that invites you to laugh? Go and visit them and 'enjoy the crack', as the Irish say.
- Do you know anyone who could do with a good dose of humour? Could you go and help them out of their malaise? Laughter loves company.

2. beliefs

In the previous chapters we have looked at your hidden beliefs about relationships, love and happiness. Here we will check out your beliefs about success. You have seen how our negative beliefs run our lives, now it's time to make these beliefs work for you in a new way.

- Remember your definition of success. Success is …
- Start to believe you are successful right now.
- Act as if you are.

This exercise will prepare you for success. Even if you cannot see the slightest sign that it's on the way, just relax. Let your Miracle Mind take over for a while. Allow it to open the way for the right job, the right relationship, the right lucky break.

Your Ego Dramatist may be going wild now, giving you every reason why this exercise won't work. The Ego Dramatist is only trying to protect you from getting hurt again. When this happens to me, I thank that part of my mind and ask it to take a break. It always works.

3. attitude

Having the right attitude is one of the basics of success. Our attitude determines the size of our dreams. It is an asset, a treasure of great value which must be protected. Beware of the vitality vampires who would love to steal your positive attitude.

As I have said before, success is a mindset, it has nothing to do with the right job or a good career. It is not about getting degrees, or the prime location for a business, or even creating a hot marketing plan. We are not successful if we are burnout and living on adrenaline.

The sole difference between success and failure is you. It is all in your attitude. Every millionaire I have spoken to about success says the single most important gift is attitude. If you have the right attitude business follows, money tags along. Attitude is a belief in yourself, attitude takes focus. You become what you think about.

- Make gratitude your attitude.
- Every day, list five things that you are grateful for.

4. give blessings

OK, I know you're not the Pope! But whenever you bless someone, you receive that blessing back tenfold. Not a bad deal? When we wish someone the best or give someone love, we feel good immediately. When we wish others success, guess what happens? It comes back to us in many different ways. Every blessing we give is a blessing we give to ourselves.

■ Close your eyes for a minute.
■ Who needs your blessing?
■ Bless them with the gift of success.
■ As you give, feel how good you feel.
■ Throughout the day carry on blessing everyone you meet.

5. enthusiasm

It's amazing how our Ego Dramatists twist everything around to give it a negative connotation. This keeps us away from one of the most powerful gifts we have: enthusiasm.

Enthusiasm is important on your ladder of success. When you are enthusiastic, you adjust yourself energetically and psychologically to receive inspiration in your work and in your life.

Once I listed the names of all the teachers, friends and work colleagues who had influenced me on my transformational path and I recognized that the gift they all willingly shared was their enthusiasm. Who do you know who has enthusiasm and willingly shares it?

You can cultivate your own unique style of enthusiasm by taking more risks in your life. This will inspire other people. Enthusiasm is contagious. It also gives you the opportunity to move beyond your fears, doubts and uncertainties and to trust the power of your Miracle Mind.

6. forgiveness

Forgiveness is another step on the success ladder. Forgiveness means letting go of pain. It finishes unfinished business and makes room for new beginnings. It releases both you and the person you have been judging or blaming. Blaming retards our growth and instantly knocks three inches off our high-heels. As you forgive you create space in your heart for someone more equal to wing their way to you. Forgiveness goes hand in hand with success – as we learn to forgive, our energy returns and so does our inner success.

- Make a list of all the trivial judgements you have made (they may be 20 years old or more).
- Start to laugh at yourself for using such trivia to hold you back from success.
- Forgive all the people you have been judging and blaming, and feel the rush of freedom.

7. permission

Giving yourself, or others, permission to be successful is a step to success not many people take. Is there anyone in your life who is waiting for your permission to be successful? As you give out permission it miraculously bounces back to you, making you successful as well. When you are successful and authentic you are also giving other people permission to be successful and authentic.

Anthony, a businessman, had become a millionaire four times over. He enjoyed working really hard for the money but then every time he got to a certain level, he'd lose the lot and have to start up again. One day he went to one of his therapists and asked the question: 'Why do I keep losing the money?' She asked him to sit down and write a list of all the people he felt he needed to get permission from: permission to be happy, permission to have a good relationship, permission to be wealthy. Anthony realized that he felt he'd never got permission from his father to be a success.

That same evening he met his father in one of the most expensive restaurants in New York. 'Dad,' he said, 'I'm asking permission to be successful.' His father laughed and said, 'But son, you *are* successful.' 'But I never asked permission, I always felt that I would be beating you, that I'd be winning against you, that I couldn't be more successful than you and that's why I let the millions go.' After this conversation they had a celebratory drink to 'success'.

As sure as eggs are eggs, Anthony become a multi-millionaire again, only this time he had permission and this time he held on to the money. Anthony is one of the most generous men I know and helps thousands of people. To him money is energy and it is in abundant supply. Every time he meets someone he gives them permission to be a millionaire by pointing them in the direction of healing and happiness.

- Would you give your partner permission to be successful?
- How about your boss? (That might be a stretch for some!)
- Do you give your offspring permission to be successful?
- How about your brothers and sisters? Are they all waiting on the sidelines, not even knowing that they are waiting for permission?
- Make a list today of all the permissions required and then grant them all. Remember, permission for success will bounce back to you too. This is a great exercise to move you on to the next level of success.

☆ success and career

The secret of a successful life is not to be found in balancing work and play so much as in integrating them. As you learn to believe in your own success, you will discover that the divide between your work and your play becomes narrower and narrower until one day it disappears altogether. What you are left with is a series of moments, some lasting for hours and others for a few seconds, but each one containing the opportunity for you to create a brand new experience of being alive. *Wear the clothes for the job you want, not the job you have.*

the path of business relationships

If you're not enjoying your job, the reason might be staring at you in the mirror.

In Chapter Five I spoke about the path of relationship from romance to conscious relationship. Career and business relationships go through the same cycles.

Think for a minute about when you first get a new job. It is great – so much potential, a new group of people, you are happy to go to work, you are going to give it your best and work hard to succeed. These are the romance and honeymoon stages.

Then, as time goes by, people in the office start to remind you of the last lot you worked with, or maybe a group you were part of years ago – the same patterns, the same gossip, the same politics. This is the shadow figure stage. Meeting the shadow figure again was probably one of the main reasons why you left your last job.

As you identify this poor shadow person, or group of people, who may not even know the feelings you have about them, you fall into the power-struggle trap. It becomes a quiet fight of wills, with you both behaving very nicely towards each other, because office etiquette doesn't allow for slanging matches. Sometimes at this stage we also bring unfinished business from our relationship at home into the office. We have just changed heads. We are heading for the zombie zone.

You can often see the zombie zone in commuters on trains – the walking dead. So many rush-hour drivers too seem to have left their bodies and emigrated to some other planet. The boredom, the burnout, the miscommunication have taken their toll, and the once inspired, passionate, enthusiastic soul is now just biding time till retirement, or secretly looking for another job.

There's no need to fall into the zombie zone. The steps to success can help make your career more than a nine-to-five drag. You could enjoy every moment, every new project, every person you meet, even the ones you may perceive as a bit quirky. You're not just on the healing path when you are meditating or doing exercises; it's there for you 24/7.

☆ success and money

The safest way to double your money is to fold it over once and put it in your pocket.

KIM HUBBARD

Success is energy, money is energy and success with money is something most people require. So how can you achieve it?

Remember that everything that you want in your life comes with its own set of underlying beliefs? That's just as true here. Money has so many negative and positive connotations that we are bound to get mixed up about it. So to get a simpler view I asked a group of ten year olds what they thought about money. Here are some of their answers:

* 'Money … always starts fights.'
* 'Money … buys me anything I want.'
* 'Money … is bad, it makes big people sad.'
* 'Money … if I'm really good I will get my allowance.'
* 'Money … I never get my spends as they always find something I did wrong.'
* 'Money … they have to keep borrowing, it's never enough.'
* 'Money … it's from the government and you don't have to work.'
* 'Money … when I grow up I will get rich and look after my mom and dad so they don't have to worry.'

Knowing what you know now about belief systems, what do you think will happen to these children when they grow up?

Until I became aware of my childhood attitudes towards money I believed you had to work 24 hours a day, seven days a week to make ends meet. This belief sabotaged my finances in many ways. I didn't love my money. I felt it was always a race against time and a struggle to stay solvent.

Today, I have a very different view of money. I now see money as an exchange of energy. I exchange energy for money when I do my work. I also exchange energy when I spend that money. This view of money has made me much more aware of the flow of energy through my life.

What are your energy levels around money? See which of these describes your situation:

survival level

At survival level we feel as though we are living on shifting sand. Insecurity and fear drain our energy and keep us from living our purpose. Money is a huge issue in our lives; we spend precious time and life energy worrying about it. We may dread answering the phone and picking up our mail.

maintenance level

At maintenance level we have a stronger foundation than at the survival level. We seem successful and earn well but always end up with more month than money. We live in a state of quiet unease and low-level stress.

abundance level

At the abundance level, our financial foundation is built on rock. We easily pay all of our lifestyle expenses and have plenty left over. We have a reserve of money and have more than enough to ride out any crisis or emergency. We have simplified our lives and decluttered our finances.

If you see yourself in level one, take comfort knowing that if you are willing to uncover your underlying beliefs and take consistent steps in the right direction, you can take your money and your life to a higher level.

If your financial foundation is level two and you want to be in level three, look at the underlying beliefs you have about success and competition. Are you competing with someone? What fears do you have about success?

Here are some questions to reflect on:

- How did your parents or guardians handle money?
- What is your earliest memory about money?
- What beliefs did you adopt as a child that are impacting on your relationship with money as an adult?
- Do they have a positive influence?
- Do they have a negative influence?

If you would know the value of money, go and try to borrow some.
BENJAMIN FRANKLIN

Jack, a telephone client, asked me to coach him on his financial situation. We went through all the different exercises and beliefs about money and success, listed his tolerations and did a whole lot of other exercises as well. Jack told me that his main issue was that he owed his father a large amount of money that his father now wanted him to repay.

When he phoned in for his next session nothing seemed to be changing in his life. This was unusual, as clients normally start to take control of their situation once they have a plan of action. I asked Jack what his Ego Dramatist had been saying. He admitted that although he had been doing the exercises on a conscious level, subconsciously he still doubted his ability to pay the debt. His Ego Dramatist had helped him to concoct a whole list of doubts and excuses. He had asked for success but had actually prepared for failure, rehearsing what he was going to say to his father when he did not repay the loan on time and thereby neutralizing all the work we had been doing together.

If you ask for success but prepare for failure, you will get the failure you prepared for.

Do you ever talk yourself out of success with money? It's all part of that racket to keep you from your greatness.

decluttering your bank balance

If you are juggling money, you are not alone. Most of the world is doing the same. Money is energy and it can pull and push. The way to money success is to know where your energy is going. Is it pulling you forward or pushing you back?

How do you talk about money; is it a friend or a foe? Many people think cash controls them, not the other way around. Rich and successful people look after their money, they have accountants to help keep an eye on it. They nurture it and understand it.

The next exercise will put you in a place of balance, with solid foundations on which you can build. I promise you these very simple steps will have a profound effect on your financial success:

When you want to start a business, most financial institutions will want you to make a business plan, a flow chart or a balance sheet. They want to know where your money comes from and where it is going.

This exercise involves drawing up a 'Karmic Balance Sheet' in your journal. Keeping a balance sheet and knowing where all your energy is going is the key to change.

■ Make an account of every single penny you owe – yes, every single penny! Include mortgage, credit-card companies, bank overdraft, car loan, store cards. As with the tolerations we described in Chapter Two, the energy attached to all your worries and bills ties you down.

- Make a second list of all the money you have borrowed from family friends and work colleagues. Go right back to your childhood and work forward to the present day. Work out what you still owe. It could be a few pence or thousands of pounds, it doesn't matter. It's still energy going out and stopping your money success. Try to phone the people or contact them in some other way to let them know you haven't forgotten about the debt.

- Do you have things you have borrowed and keep forgetting to give back? Spend time this week gathering the articles together and start to return them to their rightful owners. If you can't find the people, donate the items to someone who may be in need at this time.

- Who owes you money? Who has borrowed items from you and not returned them? Today be willing to complete this by either asking for the items or money. If you are unsure or frightened or don't know where the people are any more, be willing to let it go once and for all.

- The energy we have connected to money owed to us blocks our abundance. Test yourself here. Burn the 'money owed to you' list and see what happens to your finances within two weeks. This means you have to completely let go of any thought of the money coming back to you.

- Go through all your old purses, your pockets, your handbags, check behind the sofa and check in your old bank accounts for any spare few pounds. Become money conscious again: all these pennies add up to energy.

- Few things in life are more satisfying, uplifting and rewarding than being generous to others. You could start to give away time, money, clothes, books, even ideas. Generosity is a great step to success.

A while ago I was invited to a Pot Latch on Vancouver Island, Canada. This is a great feast that can go on for days. There is dancing and food and it's all about trust and abundance. The chief of the tribe gives everything away: pots, pans, blankets, everything. The more they give away, the more comes back to them. I'm not asking you to do that, just try giving more than you are used to. You will feel the difference inside you and it's a successful feeling.

Once you have completed your 'Karmic Balance Sheet' you can look a little more deeply into your hidden reasons for having a cash crisis. Again, be honest with yourself when answering these questions:

- What is the purpose of having your finances this way?
- What is it you are trying to prove by having your finances this way?
- Who are you taking revenge on by having your finances this way?

Every time you are having difficulty in any area of your life, ask these three questions. They could save you a lot of time and money. Then celebrate the fact that you now have control and power over your money.

☆ success and life purpose

I often think of all the times I reached my goals, fulfilled my targets, realized my dreams, only to find there was still something missing. One of my biggest mistakes was to equate success with my purpose. Success and life purpose are very different and they do not necessarily go hand in hand. Your life purpose is why you are here, whereas success is what is important to you at any particular moment in time. It is constantly changing; what was important to you yesterday may not mean so much today.

Expecting your life purpose and success to be a single entity is an ego trap that will ensnare you and hold you back. You won't be able to proceed because you will feel a failure. I know many successful healers who have healed hundreds of clients yet they believe they are failures because their practices aren't financially successful. The truth is that to be a healer is their purpose. Financial success may have to come from another direction.

☆ success and time

Know the true value of time; snatch, seize, and enjoy every moment of it. No idleness, no delay, no procrastination; never put off till tomorrow what you can do today.

LORD CHESTERFIELD

you are only 90 seconds away from success!

As children we never put anything off unless we were acting out to get attention from our parents. We were spontaneous and inspired by everything around us. As we grow older, we defer the tasks we set for ourselves, hoping that somehow they will magically do themselves. We spend hours setting goals while knowing we will never achieve them. Many a New Year's Eve I sat and listed all my New Year resolutions, only to fail within the first two weeks. I set myself up for failure every time. Now I just do everything as soon as possible and I get a great sense of achievement, especially if the task is hard.

I worked it out that the difference between success and failure can be as little as 90 seconds: the time it takes to say 'I will do it later.'

Understanding the power of the 90-second principle and using it as a tool for transformation is another way of freeing up your precious energy. You have probably noticed that to fix a problem usually takes about ten times more money and time than preventing it in the first place. Ninety seconds spent on prevention will save you stress, money and time.

When I started to write this book there were papers all over my office and lounge. It was like a dream I had years ago – death by paper. I dreamt I was drowning in words and paper, and here it was in reality, in my life. Instead of using 90 seconds to file the papers for the book, I placed them on a stack of other papers, saying to myself, 'Oh, I will know which stack they are on, no need to file them.' Of course, when I needed a particular section of the manuscript, I'd forgotten which stack it was on and it took 30 minutes of stress and anxiety frantically searching through everything else to find it.

Similarly, I decided not to write down the dates for a seminar in Switzerland because it would have 'taken too long' (about 60 seconds). The result was that I had to reschedule two seminars as the dates were double booked. Sixty seconds would have prevented this. Get the picture?

Every day you will run into situations where you can use the '90 seconds to success' principle to prevent problems and reduce stress. Ninety seconds can save a relationship: it can allow you time to think before you react to a comment. My friend Tania always says: 'Never miss an opportunity to shut up, for at least 90 seconds.'

Ninety seconds spent making a phone call now, instead of waiting, will save hours of making up stories and sometimes lies about why you didn't contact someone sooner. Ninety seconds spent saying 'I'm sorry' to somebody will save you a lifetime of regrets and heartbreak.

Last year I'd had a fight with my dad over something absolutely stupid and neither of us would give in, we were both stubborn to the end. I spent weeks in mental turmoil, going through all my letting-go exercises, trying to see him as innocent, handing him spiritual gifts from my Backpack. All those years of healing, but I was still trapped! I knew I loved him, yet my ego had me by the throat. It was the most horrible place to be: I so wanted to be right. I felt more like a nine-year-old girl than a mature woman of the world.

Finally I couldn't stand the impasse any longer. One morning I woke up really early, rang him and said, 'I'm sorry.' We had a 90-second conversation and in that time he told me he loved me and that he was sorry too. The elation we both felt after the telephone call was magic. He said, 'Come over and have a brew.' All that anguish and turmoil disappeared over a cup of tea.

- Is there anyone in your life that it's time to apologize to?
- Do you want to be right or do you want to be happy?
- Think for a minute of a person you need to say you're sorry to. It doesn't matter whether they are alive or not.
- Imagine they are standing in front of you.

- Apologize to them for what you think they did to you. Whatever you think they did to you, on one level you were doing it to them. (I did this exercise with my ex-husband Roger and it changed my life because it freed my time and my heart. It took just 90 seconds.)
- If you had no inner arguments with your loved ones going around and around your head, would that mean success to you?

☆ success and your dream

What is your dream? Does it excite you right down to the tips of your toes when you think about it? Or did you bury it long ago out of frustration? Can you remember it? Believe it or not, you were given your dream the day you strapped on your Spiritual Backpack and it's still etched onto your soul. But amnesia sets in very quickly, so maybe you've forgotten your dream.

Even if you have remembered it, let's face it, it's tough and lonely to follow your dream by yourself. A whole lot of dreams get abandoned among the weeds of resignation, rejection and fear of failure. Don't worry – your Miracle Mind is always in the background, gently guiding and nudging you along. Whether you've buried your dream or it burns brightly within you, let's get it moving.

There is no magic to realizing your dream. If you want something in life you simply have to want it totally, purely, absolutely. And more importantly, you have to *know* that you can attain it.

Believe me, this came as something of a shock after years of rubbing crystals, chanting, meditating, making success lists, buying self-help books, tapes and videos, attending and taking untold numbers of workshops and doing whatever else I could to manifest a house, a job, a man, a job, purpose, passion and adventure. Could the missing key really be so simple?

In fact we create our lives all the time. But sometimes we create a safe, secure, unexciting world in which the goal is protection. Expansion, excitement and risk-taking seem frightening, so we play small. Once you understand why you create what you don't want, you can move on to creating what you *do* want.

A dream isn't about protection and playing safe. A dream is something that inspires you to move forward. When you consider your dream you're filled with excitement and passion. You can ignite that passion through the process of visualization. Visualization is *the* most powerful life-changing process available to us.

To access the power of visualization you must evoke all your senses and emotions. Usually when people start to learn how to visualize it's as if they're looking through the lens of a camera at their little self. It's as if visualization is something outside the self. It is not! For visualization to work, you must 'feel' as if you're actually *living* your vision. By using this power repeatedly you're actually programming your subconscious to act as a compass leading you towards your dreams. Even more than that, when you use visualization *and* you pay attention to how you feel at the same time, you'll uncover your true beliefs at a gut level. Those beliefs must be in agreement with you living your dreams. You need to have your emotional, physical and mental bodies all in alignment. The moment this happens, the door to manifesting opens wide and you will have the key to attain your dream.

Next you need the courage to step out and take the action necessary to achieve your dreams. If you've spent enough time in visualization you'll be full of ideas to make your dream a reality. You'll probably experience opportunities presenting themselves to you. T.R.U.S.T. is 'To Remember Unique Sacred Timing'. Allow your Miracle Mind to lead you and listen to your intuition along the way. Keep your mind and heart open and the universe will gladly gift you your dream.

Imagination is more powerful than knowledge.
ALBERT EINSTEIN

Here's a powerful meditation on success:

▦ Take a few moments to relax. Breathe in and out fully and slowly. Feel your legs relax, feel your stomach, your arms and shoulders release and relax. Now feel your neck and jaw relax. Relax your eyes. Let go of any thoughts or concerns you may have. You can pick them up later. For now, just release them. Spend two to three minutes in this state.

▦ Picture yourself in a beautiful place in nature. You can create any type of scenery you like. Take a few moments to fully visualize the most beautiful place you can imagine. Notice the colours, the smells, the sounds. Use all of your senses and notice every detail. Do this for three to four minutes.

▦ Now that you have created your beautiful, safe and sacred place, find somewhere to sit where you can take in the warmth and radiance of the sun. The sun represents the life force. Breathe in the expansiveness of the sun. As you sit in your place of beauty, focus on the many levels of love and feel your heart expand with the joy and fullness of love. Immerse yourself in the healing power of love. Feel yourself at one with all life. Do this for about five minutes.

▦ Look at your life from a distance. See the areas in which you would like more success. How would you like your life to look and feel when you are expressing your highest vision? Spend five or six minutes fully visualizing this.

▦ Now ask for guidance on your next step towards manifesting this. Stay in the feeling of love for a further four or five minutes.

▦ Give thanks and send out blessings to all beings.

▦ Write down any impressions or thoughts in your journal.

When you finally begin to live your dream you will be swept away. Nature will force you to become a more powerful person. Although you will have days when your expectations aren't met and you feel as though nothing is working, this is just your Ego Dramatist vying for power over your Miracle Mind. However, the days of blessed wonder will far exceed the down days, because in that deep soul place miracles really can happen.

☆ remember *success* is already hidden in your spiritual backpack!

To recap, remember success is a gift to you from heaven. It is the ability to transform boredom into adventure, fear into love and guilt and fear into trust. Success is different things to different people. It's knowing what makes *you* feel successful that is the key to your success. In reality we are all successful.

Success and creativity are your gifts to the world. Creativity is love made manifest. Showing the world that you are an original masterpiece is the last step on the High-Heeled Healer's journey. But first have some more fun in the office …

☆ healerette's happy hour

* Make a point of greeting everyone in a very friendly way as you come into the office/shop/workplace. (If you see someone without a smile, give them yours.)
* Find something to compliment each of your workmates on.
* Take in a large box of biscuits or chocolates and share them around.
* In a meeting, suggest that you take five minutes for everyone's 'utterly ridiculous ideas' – often the most creative ideas come when people stop trying to be sensible.
* Pin your favourite cartoon on your computer or notice-board or buy a plant or put a favourite crystal near your computer terminal – anything that will brighten up and personalize the place where you spend so much of your time.

Chapter Seven

creativity

Your vision will become clear only when you look into your heart... Who looks outside, dreams. Who looks inside, awakens.
CARL GUSTAV JUNG

When I decided to write this book I looked around desperately for my muse. I sat and cried for many an hour, believing I hadn't one single thought that was my own. I had enough blocks to build a pyramid! It took me ages to realize that I was giving my power away. My Ego Dramatist had taken over yet again. The Ego Dramatist always seems to catch us at the point when we are ready to step up in our lives. Here it was blocking my creativity.

Like many people I thought that you had to have studied arduously in a specific area such as music, art or literature, or be perfect in some special way before you could dare class yourself as 'creative'. Yet creativity is our true nature. It is a lot like dreaming. We don't know how we do it, we just do it. When creativity flows, the information comes to us through our senses and we are inspired and touched by a spirited energy, something much bigger than ourselves.

To be creative you simply need to use your imagination, your vision, and get in touch with your enchanted self, so creating something unique from within yourself. It is OK to be inspired and fired with enthusiasm from others – creativity does not happen in a vacuum. Your purpose is to find that *one spark* that can create *your* masterpiece.

You may have always wanted to write a bestselling novel or paint your own masterpiece, knit a colourful cardie, design a fantastic floral display or create that one special recipe with your own secret ingredients. Or have you ever thought about starting up your own business? Doing something you love to do and making a living? You have to be creative to get the idea from the drawing-board to the bank manager's office and then get even more creative with the figures. There are a million ways to be creative and each one is as unique as we are. If you choose, you could start to live your life today from a creative perspective, to look at adversities differently, to embrace the precious gifts hidden behind any problem, to learn to rise above the storms and fly.

It's time to open up your intuitive mind. The mind is your servant, not your master. If you ask the right questions, you will get the right answers. If you are prepared to listen to your Miracle Mind, with its connection to heaven, it will bring all the information you need to create your wildest dreams. Yet you may still be using your racket to block your giftedness. If you are feeling mad, bad or sad for any reason, your creative juices will get tangled in your racket strings and find it harder to flow. In this chapter, we will remove a few more strings from your racket.

☆ remember those rackets

Nestled in the mountains of southern Spain is a magical village to which many artists have decided to relocate. They originate from Britain, France, Holland, Germany, Italy and the USA. One thing they have in common is the wish to emigrate to the sun and create an entirely new life – learning a new language, trying out new food and making new friends. They all want more time to enjoy their lives, to start again, to leave a rat race where the rats are winning. This community has evolved over 15 years. The villagers live in an assortment of dwellings, farms, villas and apartments and in one case even a wigwam – the whackier the better. There are painters, musicians, healers, fashion designers, writers and actors all living in this little piece of paradise.

For a long time people find this idyllic spot is as close to heaven as you can possibly get. The weather is perfect and in the evenings they feel as if they can touch the stars. Tax is low and food and wine are cheap. Their creativity positively blossoms. However, one by one, many of them start to close down their creative connection. What they don't realize is that when they are packing to leave for paradise they are neatly tucking their rackets into their suitcases as well.

I have been lucky enough to facilitate many workshops in this peaceful oasis. The workshops are never the same. The humour, fun, tears and emotions are phenomenal. When I work, I use puppets and props, in fact anything that is to hand. At one workshop I had four 'Healerettes' travelling with me as assistants: they were all healers, therapists and most of all friends. In the seminar room were 45 gorgeous beings all eager to release the old misunderstandings that had been blocking their creativity. I explained to the group that the seminar is process-led rather than programmed. (A programmed workshop has an itinerary with a scheduled timetable to go through; with a process-led workshop the Miracle Mind leads the way and we follow.) I warned them that on many occasions when I am working with people who are releasing old misunder-standings, just at the point of letting go doors have slammed shut for no apparent reason or lights have flickered. Sometimes birds or butterflies not normally seen in that area have flown in and then out again. You might consider that a bit spooky, but the workshops allow us to realize how connected we are to everything around us, and that is a reassuring thought.

are you feeling mad, bad or sad?

The three emotions that hold back a tide of creativity are being *mad* at someone or feeling *bad* and *sad*. These are the good, the bad and the ugly of emotional blocks. However, they are not wholly negative; many great masters have felt a deep sadness and have dug deep into their psyche to pull out nuggets of gold which they have shared with the world. These exercises are about finding an easier way.

feeling mad ...

Marita, a 75-year-old former actress from Germany, attended the workshop because her painting skills seemed to be drying up. She told me that all her life the person she had been most *mad* at was her mother. When I asked why, she told me her mother had wanted her to be a ballet dancer. For most of her formative years she had practised long and hard to fulfil her mother's dream. But as a result of many injuries, her health had suffered and although she reached the *corps de ballet* she never succeeded in becoming a prima ballerina and had to retire at 18 with damaged feet.

Marita had packed this old pain tightly into her racket: it had been there for over 60 years. I asked her if she knew what the gift was that she hadn't shared with her mother due to the fact she had been mad at her for so long? Marita thought for a while then said very tentatively, with a little glint of the rebel in her eye, 'Success, but how can I give her that gift now, she has been dead for years?' I explained that it didn't matter if the person we had the fight with had already used their return ticket and left the planet. All that mattered was that Marita understood, accepted and forgave her mother's behaviour and moved on with her own life. Then she would have fulfilled her purpose of giving this gift of success to her mum.

Marita went on to explain that her mother had come from a war-torn part of Europe. Her dream had been to be a ballerina herself, but it was impossible at that time. I asked Marita to look around the room and choose somebody from the group who would represent her mother. She chose a statuesque French lady who apparently was a double for her mother when she was in her prime. I then asked Marita what a prima ballerina would wear that a ballet dancer wouldn't. She replied, 'A tiara.' To her surprise, and the Healerettes', I had actually packed a child's Cinderella-style tiara in my case! (I must admit that it's not something I normally carry around with me. When I'm preparing for a workshop, I don't know what the issues are going to be, so I just go with the process. I don't know why or how these seemingly silly items are going to work, but creativity and synchronicity often take a hand in the healing process.) I then asked Marita if she would be prepared to give the gift of success to her 'mum'. Her eyes lit up and you could see years of pain fall away. 'Yes, of course I would.' I gently placed the tiara on her head and asked her to go to the person representing her mother.

Seventy-five-year-old Marita decided to dance the 'Dance of the Dying Swan' in honour of her dead mother, and give her the gift of success at last. She had remembered it step by step and gave her best performance in honour of her mother. There wasn't a dry eye in the house. We all cried as we looked at this graceful older lady who had taken all those years to become a prima ballerina at last.

Since then, Marita has created the most amazing paintings of the dying swan and started writing a novel based on her life. Her health has also improved tremendously. She now drives around the village wearing her tiara and giving the royal wave to all the locals.

Like Marita's, every block has a story attached to it. It's an elaborate trick of the Ego Dramatist designed to prove us right about another person's behaviour. The story interrupts the silence and the stillness we need to become inspired, motivated and enthusiastic about life again.

Ask yourself these questions:

- Who are you still mad at?
- What is the gift hiding behind the story?

- Would you be prepared to make the person more important than the story?
- Would you be prepared to give the gift and create an abundant healthy life?

feeling bad ...

Have you ever done something and then felt really bad inside? Have you ever felt bad about hurting somebody? Do you have to be right all the time? Is it hindering your ability to get on with your life?

Peter, a tall, good-looking Swedish doctor, had recently retired. He told me that he had felt bad for nearly 15 years, since the last time he saw his eldest son Steven. I asked what had happened to cause this rift. He told me that he and his son were exact duplicates, like two peas in a pod; people said they were more like brothers than father and son. They had gone fishing, skiing, sailing and played ice hockey together. But then arguments had started and tempers flared constantly.

Over time, the relationship became extremely fraught and the pair could hardly stay in the same room. On his eighteenth birthday, Steven had left home and they hadn't spoken since, although Steven kept in touch with his mother, who was also on the workshop. She explained that Peter was very, very competitive and had to win at all costs; he always had to be right. His son hadn't wanted to be in competition with his father so had often lost on purpose, but eventually it all just got too much for him. Peter didn't know how to stop his feelings bubbling up, he felt bad about his behaviour towards his son and wanted to heal that relationship more than anything in the world.

Emotions such as mad, bad and sad are only feelings: they come and then go. They are meant to be felt – after all, we choose to come to this planet in the first place to learn how to feel. As you get more in touch with your feelings, you can learn to deal appropriately with things that upset you. You don't have to be afraid of feelings. The best thing to do with uncomfortable feelings is to just watch and be aware of them; to learn from them. Call them by name: 'I'm feeling sad and hurt right now!' 'I feel bad and down.' 'I feel mad about…' By learning to identify and accept your feelings you can learn to drop your anxiety and defensive behaviour. As you let go of your need to control and compete with others, you have more energy to spend on the things that are important to you. Life is more fun when you no longer have to be in competition with the world.

I asked Peter to do the following exercise. Here are his answers:

- Close your eyes and imagine you are carrying two suitcases and in each suitcase there is the competition that you have with everyone around you.
- How big are the cases? … *'Very, very big.'*
- Are they heavy or light? … *'Extremely heavy.'*
- How much would they weigh? … *'Twenty kilos each.'*
- How many people are you in competition with? … *'Everyone.'*
- How old is this competition? … *'Old.'*
- Who is the first person you were in competition with? … *'My brother Mateus.'*
- OK, now can you imagine putting down these cases filled with competition?
- Start to feel the true power coming back into your life. Ask your Miracle Mind to put you, and everybody you have been in competition with, into a peaceful place where it is light and safe. Creativity flows when we have a sense of safety and self-worth.
- Imagine giving Mateus a gift. What would it be? … *'Freedom.'*
- As the universal energy believes in fair exchange, what does Mateus have for you? … *'My son.'*
- Would you accept your son in all his greatness? … *'Yes.'*
- Can you ask your Miracle Mind to find your son and ask him to be willing to talk to you? … *'Yes.'*
- What is your son saying to you? … *'I love you, Dad.'*
- Can you forgive yourself this misunderstanding and choose to join your son? … *'Yes.'*
- How does that feel? … *'Wonderful.'*

After the exercise Peter realized it was years since he had felt so good. He decided to make plans to meet up with his 'prodigal son' as soon as possible. His wife told me later that with his renewed energy and his son back in the fold, Peter had also spoken to his brother Mateus and healed another string in his racket.

feeling sad ...

In the deepest part of the mind we are all longing to go back home. We came here to wake up the world and to share and receive gifts, although many of us don't fulfil our purpose and are still asleep. And if we aren't fulfilling our purpose we will have an underlying feeling of sadness.

Spirituality means waking up. Many come to Earth and fall fast asleep. They are born asleep, live asleep, marry in their sleep and even die in their sleep. They never wake up. They never quite understand their purpose and their mystical connection. But without this connection to spirit, this dream planet can be more like a nightmare.

I heard this funny story a few years ago whilst working in South Africa.

A women knocked on her son's door. 'Philip,' she called, 'wake up, it's eight and it's late.' Philip answered, 'I don't want to go to school.' 'Why not?' asked the mother. 'Three reasons,' says Philip. 'First because it's soooo dull, second the kids all tease me and third, I hate school.' His mother replied, 'Well, I'm going to tell you three reasons why you must go to school. First, because you chose that school, second because you are nearly 40 years old and third because you are the head teacher. It's time to wake up!'

Many of us are like this. All we see are the problems, not the adventures. We are frightened of being teased because we are different from the other sleepwalkers and also we are the teachers of a new paradigm. We carry a wealth of spiritual gifts to feed the hungry souls and spirits of the world, yet we procrastinate and act small.

Serena said she had no good reason to feel sad, her life seemed to be working just as she had visualized it. She said that over the years she had spent a small fortune on personal development seminars which had helped her and her partner of 26 years to understand the bigger picture of life. Serena had two children who were well-balanced, independent individuals who had their own lives away from their parents. Her motive for attending my workshop was to get to the bottom of this deep soulful sadness that she couldn't seem to clear.

After speaking to Serena about her vision for life, it turned out that the underlying sadness was due to the fact that she didn't really believe she could ever fulfil her ambition to teach spirituality in business. She wanted to take all the metaphysical knowledge she held and create a training model that would be business-friendly.

I asked Serena what she taught at the moment and she replied, 'Confidence and self-esteem.' Many years ago I was told by my old teacher that we always teach what we need to learn. I mentioned this to Serena and she laughed her socks off. 'So how long have you been playing this role of the confident business trainer?' I asked. 'Years!' she replied. She told me that her biggest fear was that one day everybody would find out she was playing a role and this also made her feel sad and a fraud.

I asked Serena to relax and close her eyes for a moment, allowing her Miracle Mind to help heal the situation. Try this exercise with Serena:

- If your sadness were a person, who would it be? ... *'My daughter.'*
- What is the gift you have for your daughter at this time? ... *'Confidence.'*
- Give her the gift of confidence, what is happening now? ... *'She's smiling.'*
- In your mind's eye, go and join her. Give her a big hug. ... *'Hmm, that feels good.'*
- What do you need most in your life at this time? ... *'Love and forgiveness from my daughter. I seemed to always be working. I feel guilty for not being a better mother. This makes me feel so sad because all I wanted to do was give her the best.'*

- Imagine your daughter giving you the gift of love and forgiveness. Could you receive that from her? ... Serena gently smiled and nodded.
- Can you ask for heaven's help to give confidence to everyone around you, including yourself? ... *'Yes, I sure can.'*

Serena had been judging herself constantly and sabotaging her career. Now she was free to take steps to fulfil her purpose of bringing heart and soul into the business world.

- What dream are you frightened of fulfilling?
- What is your Ego Dramatist telling you?
- Who needs your help at this moment in time?
- Think of that person and send them love, compassion, confidence – whatever you intuitively know they need. Whatever you think they need is exactly what you will receive from the universe for your journey.
- Are you ready to receive this help?

It's time now to take a break; all you need for this exercise is a pen and your journal.

Expressive art and performing art are two very different modes of creativity. Performing art is for the gallery or the stage. It has an end product which is usually to please the critics and the audience. Expressive art is more concerned with the process than the end result.

Now it's your turn to get expressive. Have you ever tried creative doodling as an expressive healing tool? This kind of doodling is about letting your feelings come through you and onto paper. No words, no thinking, no agenda. Just let your feelings spill on to the page. Hold the pen in your non-dominant hand and let your intuitive mind take over for a while. You may be pleasantly surprised at your mini-masterpiece.

☆ ask yourself the right questions

How many times have you asked the question: 'Why is my creativity blocked?' Let's suppose you could listen to all the thoughts running around in your head. Pretend for a minute you also have a special microphone that could convert your thoughts into spoken words. What would your thoughts sound like? For many people, they would sound like this:

★ Why am I so ★★★★?
★ Why am I such a ★★★★?
★ Why am I always ★★★★?
★ Why am I so afraid of ★★★★?

But these negative questions are actually part of the reason you are not allowing your creativity to flow. Think of a question you are always asking yourself. You know the one, it is like an obsessive mantra or sentence in your head. Write it down in your journal.

If you asked a negative question, you will always get a negative answer. This is because you have subconsciously asked your brain to find backup from your inner data bank. For example, if you ask: 'Why am I frightened of change?', your brain will immediately provide you with all the proof you need to reinforce the belief that you are frightened of change.

What questions are you used to hearing from yourself? Are they motivating and inspiring or negative and unsupportive? If your questions sabotage you rather than support you, you are brainwashing yourself, setting yourself up to fail before you even start your marvellous creative project. But what are your reasons? Bring the dark gremlin words of failure out into the open. Write them down in your journal and clear some space in your mind.

your Oprah Winfrey interview

Imagine you are invited onto *The Oprah Winfrey Show*. Oprah is so impressed by your creative skills that she asks: 'Why are you so creative? How did you start? What's your next project?' You are so taken aback you ask the question out loud to yourself: 'Hmmm, why … am … I … so … *creative…?*'

Not only has the question surprised you, it has shocked your brain as well. You have never asked yourself a question quite like that before. You have been programmed *not* to shine. You have been so embarrassed about your Spiritual Backpack being full of creativity that you have had to hide it under years of negative thought patterns.

Now ask yourself again: 'Why am I so creative? *Why am I so creative?*' Do you know what your brain is doing now? It is finding the answers to the question you just asked. It is diligently searching its data bank for proof that you *are* creative.

Try some more positive questions:

- 'Why am I such a good … mum/dad/lover/wife/husband/boss/friend?'
- 'Why am I so … creative/loving/helpful?'
- 'What am I gifted at?' (Don't be shy here.)

Are you surprised by the answers? Be positive about them. Keep your mind open to all the new possibilities. Write down the results in your journal.

When I first tried this exercise my Ego Dramatist negated the intuitive process, loudly and clearly trying to prevent my transformation. Here's what I heard: 'It can't be that easy. Who are you kidding? There is no hidden information. Intuition? That's only for mystics.' I wrote all the ego chatter down, cleared my mind and trusted it would work. And guess what? It did!

What other questions would you like answers to? What questions have you been too shy to ask? Go on, ask. What have you got to lose? Have some fun with this process. Write it all in your journal, your private space.

finding intuition

All these exercises have relied on you using your intuition. Intuition is your internal information; it is an inner library of physical and emotional signs. It is your inner teacher. The ego has trained us to discount or repress this internal voice and therefore neglect it, devalue it or refuse to recognize its message. Intuition and creativity illuminate; they bring the light of love and help you to show your gifts to the world. You have every answer you ever needed in your head, all you have to do is start to trust and ask different questions. Minds are very similar to parachutes; they are packed very tight into a small space but once they open they work wonderfully. Keep that wonderful mind open, as you did when you were a child. You are waking up to your greatness. Happy intuiting.

finding inspiration

As a healer and a success coach, I have a varied toolbox. But a while ago I wanted to be more creative around healing and transformation so I sat and asked myself the question: 'What would be a unique way to clear hidden blocks?' Within a few minutes an idea started to form. I decided to take my groups to a car-boot sale or flea market for some shopping, some good old-fashioned retail therapy, in a way that would be inexpensive, fun and healing. This is how my unique 'Shamanic Shopping' process was created.

The group arrives at the car-boot sale or flea market and everyone pairs up with a designated buddy. We then set off to buy two specific objects. One object should remind you of somebody or something from the past you want to let go of and the other object should represent what you want to manifest in your life now. There is a spending limit of five pounds. Everybody also buys simple little gifts to share with the other participants. This form of creative healing works miraculously. It is fun, unique and we even get some bargains in the process. We all have a fantastic shopping and healing time and when the group gets back together we have a hot chocolate and a croissant and the atmosphere is similar to a childhood Christmas. Everyone is thrilled to share the insights they have gleaned during their shopping trip and to give their gifts. When I ask people how they feel doing this unique exercise, everybody replies, 'Happy, excited, inspired, creative.' I tell them the reason they are so high is that they are living life on purpose and sharing their gifts with others.

Another creative form of healing and fun is when I ask participants on my 'Shirley Valentine Experience' seminars to bring food to share from the country they would love to run away to. In these seminars we work with the problems that occur in any relationship. I explain the anatomy of a problem and how to heal it. Let's look at this now.

creative problem-solving

When a problem occurs it's usually because of our split mind: the conscious mind wants to move forward, but the subconscious mind is afraid of losing something or someone to which we are attached. We then project this fear onto a person or situation which seems to obstruct us. So we have a good reason to fight with someone. It looks as though they're the 'baddie' stopping us from getting on with our lives, when in fact we are setting them up.

Have you ever thought what the anatomy of a problem would look like? This is a model I was taught many years ago by Dr Chuck Spezzano, a teacher of mine.

Imagine a triangle with each side representing part of a problem:

1. Illusions
2. Grievances
3. Holding on

Heal any one side of the triangle and the triangle, and the problem, will collapse.

illusions

An illusion is a refusal to see others as they really are. Instead of seeing them as beautiful, creative, energetic beings just like us, we start to project our guilty feelings onto them and see them as bad, inadequate, wrong and so forth. The same applies to groups, races, organizations, countries. Blame and separation are impossible without illusion.

To collapse illusions, ask yourself these questions (and listen to your intuitive answers):

- What am I projecting on to others that I feel guilty about? (Jealousy is a good one to try out – have you ever been jealous of a partner when you yourself are starting to window shop for a new mate? You start blaming them for what you are already doing.)
- Can I help the person I am projecting guilt onto and free myself from this block? (You don't have to wash, cook and clean or go on your knees to them. All you have to do is take responsibility for your part in the fight and to see them as innocent.)
- Can I let them off the hook?

grievances

Grievances are another great trap. They are another form of holding on to where we still have a broken heart. There's no room for miracles and magic and enchantment in our lives because we're still holding on to a silly old grievance!

- Is there anyone I still have a grievance with?
- What talent, gift or opportunity am I pushing away by keeping this story going?
- Try the five-word process. *Could you* let it go? *Would you* let it go? *When*?

holding on

The holding-on side of the problem triangle is a great excuse not to be creative. We hold on to past pain, past lifestyle, past successes and past failures. Ninety per cent of the pain you feel when you have a problem has been dragged from the past into the present. When you are stuck in the past, it serves a purpose for you, you are using it to justify a certain behaviour in the present. But the past is over, it doesn't exist any more, it is only kept alive by the Ego Dramatist. All this holding on stops you taking the next step in your life. If you are still holding on to something, your mind will think you still have it and it will get in the way of being able to create a better life.

- What great creative disaster are you still holding on to? (It could be from as far back as the first years at school when your fantastic painting of great big purple dragon with green eyes surrounded by pink, yellow and black trees was frowned on by your teacher. Allow your Miracle Mind to help you with this question.)
- What would happen if you let go of this problem? Your life could transform in the blink of an eye.

As well as these exercises, you can collapse the problem triangle by using any of the exercises throughout the book. Ask yourself which side of the triangle would be the most difficult to deal with and then concentrate on healing that part. This is an effective and creative way of problem-solving. And remember to have fun along the way!

Creativity lives in paradox: Serious art is born from serious play.
JULIA CAMERON, AUTHOR OF *The Artist's Way*

☆ healerette's happy hour

Today when I go into bookshops and metaphysical stores I see shelves packed with tarot cards, medicine cards, angel cards, all kinds of divination packs. How about making your own special exclusive deck of healing cards based on all the exercises in the book? Your own personal deck will be unique to you and therefore very, very powerful. The cards will be your creation, with your own specific issues in them. You can use them if you are looking for instant answers or need some inspiration; you can use them on your own or with your friends; but most of all, have fun with them.

You can make an elaborate deck if you wish or just use pieces of paper that could be kept in an envelope to carry in your purse. I do this sometimes with my groups and it gives me great delight to watch them lying on the floor with their colouring pens and paper – whether they are 15 years old or 75! It's like watching a miracle spread across the carpet magically opening the doorway to a new reality. After all the seriousness of doing all the exercises and healing the rackets of a lifetime, this a fun way to construct a new life with new values, beliefs and dreams.

Start off with three suits, each with a different focus:

* Your Gifts suit
* Your Traps suit
* Your Healing suit

the gifts suit

Start by listing all the gifts you have in your unique Spiritual Backpack. Remember you can always call on the Miracle Mind, which is full of love and grace, to bring in more gifts that you would like in your life. Don't be shy, you can manifest anything. Write your gifts down on separate index cards or paper. This is *your* Gifts suit. Colour the back of these cards in the most vibrant colours of the rainbow.

Some Gifts suit ideas:

Inspiration, Acceptance, Patience, Humour, Beauty, Health , Love, Sexuality, Spontaneity, Creativity, Simplicity, Confidence, Success, Generosity, Balance, Wealth, Vitality, Happiness, Romance, Peace, Silence, Grace, Compassion, Wisdom, Reflection, Understanding, Homemaking, Excellence, Surrender, Choice, Trust, Joy, Flow, Manifesting, Abundance, Enthusiasm, Authenticity, Innocence, Freedom…

The list goes on and on… If you get stuck, just get in touch with your Miracle Mind and it will connect you back up to heaven.

the traps suit

Next start to list all the problems you may have unearthed while working through the book, all the issues that you keep stumbling over time and again. Perhaps you'd like to write these in black ink. Check back through your journal – you may find some old juicy ones. The backs of this suit could be in a dark colour or could be a spider's web or anything else that represents a deep, dark space to you.

Ideas for your Traps suit:

Vampiring, Clutter Buts, Tolerations, Swamp Queen, Heartbreak, Neediness, Eeyore, Jealousy, Family Roles, Hero, Martyr, Lost Child, Scapegoat,

Entertainer, Independent, Dependant, Sabotage, Fear, Guilt, Revenge, Gossip, Worry, Regrets, Holding On, Complaints, Feeling Sad, Bad, Mad, Expectations, Lemon Lips, Zombie Zone, Mind-Reading, Calculator Trap, Doubt, Power Struggle, Stubbornness, Being Right, Drama Queen, Judgement, Blame…

Have fun looking back over your exercises and laughing at the silliness of it all.

the healing suit

Now for the lovely Healing suit. What exercises did you like best in the book? Only use the ones that resonated with you; that way healing is easy, as it is meant to be.

Here are some ideas:

Choice, Accountability, Letting Go, Forgiveness, True Communication, Joining, Miracle Mindedness, Giving Gifts, Sharing, Decluttering, Visualizing a Happy Life, Sending Blessings, Understanding, Acceptance, Reassurance, Spirit Talk, Creating a Masterpiece…

These cards could be coloured with the gentlest of colours or even backed with cashmere or flower petals – anything that represents healing to you.

how to use your deck

Use the cards however you wish, or however you would use a more conventional pack. Perhaps you could ask an intuitive question such as 'What is the block that is holding me back?' Pull a card from your Traps suit. Then pull out a Healing card to show you the way through. It will represent an exercise you know well. Finally, pull out one of your Gift cards.

Gifts are what the whole book has been about and now it's time to receive those that are being offered to you. Enjoy them and watch how the universal energy takes you on the journey of a lifetime, full of purpose, passion and adventure.

taking the next steps

I feel that I am on a path that is still unfolding. The way in which my career has developed has made me marvel at the ease and grace with which life just flows at times – if we allow it to. I now teach throughout Europe, South Africa, Australia and the UK. I facilitate seminars onboard a Caribbean cruise ship. And I have had the honour of working with the First Nation tribes on the reservations in northern British Columbia, Canada. I have taught lawyers and labourers, craftsmen and CEOs, surgeons and sailors, mothers and models – in fact, anyone who is ready to become more daring and authentic.

Now you too can take the next steps on your journey of purpose, passion and adventure. Who knows what lies ahead of you? I have always been amazed at the results once we learn to access the hidden parts of our hearts and minds and uncover the gifts we've buried there, sometimes for lifetimes. It's never to late to reconnect to heaven and give your gifts to the world. And the world will give you gifts in return.

Having reached this far on your journey, you will have looked into your heart and awakened many possibilities there for change. As you step forward towards your greatness, be aware that coincidence and synchronicities will be sent by heaven to guide you. And remember that life is meant to be fun! Enjoy it!

I wish you success and happiness on your journey of adventure.

author biography

High-Heeled Healer Ann Marie Woodall specializes in the psychology of relationships and transformation. She lectures and teaches in the UK, Europe, South Africa and Australia, and has successfully taken her powerful and innovative approach to healing and humour into Canada, working with the First Nations tribes, gaining insight into their culture, spirituality and shamanic practice, which she has integrated into her model of healing.

Her seminars are innovative and creative. She uses fun, laughter and safety to create a sacred place for healing and for exploring your natural gifts, often hidden even from yourself, combining a unique blend of insight, spirituality and humour. This book and her work will touch, motivate and inspire anyone who has ever said 'There has got to be more to life than this'.

For more information on talks, seminars, corporate training and a calendar of events, see www.highheeledhealer.com or call 01903 717776 during office hours.

Make
www.thorsonselement.com
your online sanctuary

Get online information, inspiration and guidance to help you on the path to physical and spiritual well-being. Drawing on the integrity and vision of our authors and titles, and with health advice, articles, astrology, tarot, a meditation zone, author interviews and events listings, www.thorsonselement.com is a great alternative to help create space and peace in our lives.

So if you've always wondered about practising yoga, following an allergy-free diet, using the tarot or getting a life coach, we can point you in the right direction.

www.thorsonselement.com

thorsons
element